MERCY
REVEALED

MERCY REVEALED

A Cross-Centered Look at Christ's Miracles

Gerald M. Bilkes

Reformation Heritage Books
Grand Rapids, Michigan

Mercy Revealed
© 2015 by Gerald M. Bilkes

Reformation Heritage Books
2965 Leonard St. NE
Grand Rapids, MI 49525
616–977–0889 / Fax 616–285–3246
orders@heritagebooks.org
www.heritagebooks.org

Printed in the United States of America
15 16 17 18 19 20/10 9 8 7 6 5 4 3 2 1

Library of Congress Cataloging-in-Publication Data

Bilkes, Gerald M.
  Mercy revealed : a cross-centered look at Christ's miracles /
Gerald M. Bilkes.
     pages cm
  Includes bibliographical references.
  ISBN 978-1-60178-409-4 (pbk. : alk. paper) 1. Jesus Christ—Miracles—Biblical teaching. 2. Bible. Gospels—Criticism, interpretation, etc. I. Title.
  BT366.3B55 2015
  226.7'06—dc23
                            2015016013

For additional Reformed literature, request a free book list from Reformation Heritage Books at the above regular or e-mail address.

For my children,

Lauren, Seth, Zach, Audrey, and Josh,
all of whom greet me daily as miracles of God.

I pray that each of you will experience the
greatest miracle of all—being drawn into fellowship
with God, through Christ, the Son of God.

Contents

Acknowledgments

After the publication of a book on the parables of Jesus, *Glory Veiled and Unveiled*, I was encouraged to write a sequel on the miracles of Jesus, which I started to do more years ago than I would care to admit. For many different reasons, the project stalled a number of times, and it is largely because of the persistent encouragement and loving prodding of Jay Collier of Reformation Heritage Books that this book crossed the finish line.

I also want to thank Annette Gysen from RHB for her invaluable editing and comments, which helped better the book immensely. Steve Renkema, David Woollin, Amy Zevenbergen, Linda den Hollander, and the other staff at RHB all deserve thanks for their contributions, along with Dr. Joel Beeke for agreeing to publish it. An initial draft of these chapters appeared in installments in *The Banner of Sovereign Grace Truth* and *The Messenger*, and I am grateful to the respective editors, Dr. Joel Beeke and Rev. Cornelis Pronk, for permission to publish them in this format.

A special thanks goes to Michelle, who, besides being a constant help and stay for me and for our children, frequently helps by editing my work—filling in the gaps, connecting the dots, and straightening out the logic.

Thanks also to Kate DeVries, my sister-in-law, for her edits, as well as to my father, Dr. Lawrence Bilkes, and brother, Rev. Lawrence J. Bilkes, for providing helpful comments on many of the chapters. Thanks also to my research assistants and others who have helped see this book through—Rev. Michael Borg, Kenneth Hutton, Ryan Hurd, and Marjoleine deBlois—all of whom worked readily and cheerfully for me. Any remaining errors are my own responsibility, though all of them have saved me from many more.

I want to acknowledge my colleagues in the Free Reformed Churches, with whom I am privileged to labor, as well as the Theological Education Committee of the FRC, under whose oversight I serve. I also want to thank my seminary colleagues, Dr. Michael Barrett, Dr. Joel Beeke, Rev. Mark Kelderman, Dr. David Murray, and Dr. William Van-Doodewaard, who are a source of daily encouragement and inspiration to me. Finally, I wish to thank the Son of God, who alone does wondrous things.

Introduction: Learning about Christ from His Miracles

Luke 7:19–23

Jesus...said unto them, Go your way, and tell John what things ye have seen and heard; how that the blind see, the lame walk, the lepers are cleansed, the deaf hear, the dead are raised, to the poor the gospel is preached.

—LUKE 7:22

This is a study of the miracles of Christ as they are recorded by the gospel writers Matthew, Mark, and Luke.[1] Christ's miracles are not the only ones recorded in Scripture. We are given detailed accounts of miracles in the Old Testament, especially in the accounts of Moses, Elijah, and Elisha. The opening pages of the New Testament also record miracles such as the birth of John the Baptist and the conception of Jesus Christ. After Christ's ascension, His disciples performed many notable miracles. Miracles were not something that occurred only during biblical times. Christ still performs miracles both as He saves sinners and sustains His people every day. As He carries them, heals them, restores them, and delivers them from their fears, He is working out His perfect plan, filled as it is with countless miracles. However, the miracles Christ performed Himself while He walked this earth are perhaps the most well known and beloved by Christians.

But I do not want us to study these miracles only because they are loved or well known. They are also valuable because of what they teach us about Christ. Peter made an important point about these miracles on the day of Pentecost: "Jesus of Nazareth, a man approved of God among you by miracles and wonders and signs, which God did by him in the midst of you, as ye yourselves also know" (Acts 2:22). The miracles magnify Christ's glory, pointing to Him as one approved by God. If Christ has His Father's approval, how can He not be worthy of ours?

Defining Miracles

The miracles of Christ were special signs that He performed during His public ministry. He did things that others could not do—things that proved that God was with Him, as Nicodemus noted (John 3:2). These events ran counter to expected natural processes.

In a certain sense, everything God does is a miracle. For example, many miracles were involved in His creation of heaven and earth in six days. God's upholding everything by His providence is a miracle. The sunshine and rain, the springtime and harvest, and many other natural phenomena point to the might and power of God, who works in ways we cannot trace (Eccl. 11:5). Yet, as we will see, the Bible speaks specifically of miracles and, in doing so, refers to events that distinguish themselves from normal and expected processes.

The Bible uses three main words for miracles. Each one emphasizes a certain aspect of the miraculous character of an event. In many instances, only one of the three words is used in a narrative. But in Acts 2:22, as Peter describes Christ's miracles, all three of the words are in the same verse.

The first word used by Peter and in other passages is *dunamis*, or "powerful deed." This word stresses the might or power required for the performance of a miracle. For example, Christ used this word when He said, "If the mighty works had been done in Tyre and Sidon, which have been done in you, they had a great while ago repented" (Luke 10:13).

Teras, or "wonder," is the second word that is used. It emphasizes the response required by or expected from the miracle. A person witnessing or hearing about the event ought to be amazed. This word is used in John 4:48: "Except ye see signs and wonders, ye will not believe."

Third is *semeion*, or "sign." In other words, the miracle serves as a signal or signpost, pointing the person who sees it or hears of it to something else. This word is used in John 20:30: "And many other signs truly did Jesus in the presence of his disciples."

The Kinds of Miracles

Biblical scholars have attempted to categorize the miracles into groups. One common method classifies them according to who or what is involved, as follows:

- *Miracles involving human beings*: This is the most common kind of miracle in the Gospels. Christ cured people with diseases and even brought the dead back to life. Some were healed with a touch, others from a distance. In each case, it was clear that Christ was the source of healing. Miracles involving demon-possessed people could be included as a subcategory within this group.

- *Miracles involving creation or nature*: The well-known miracles in which there is a calming of the sea, walking on water, or multiplying of loaves and fishes are included in this group. Something within the created order was being acted upon and became subservient to its Creator in a new and incredible way.

The Purposes of the Miracles

Why did Christ perform miracles on earth? Luke 9:19–23 helps us answer this question. While in prison, John the Baptist sent his disciples to ask Jesus whether He was the promised Messiah, or if they had to wait for someone else. In answer to his question, Christ sent the disciples back to John with reports of the miracles He was performing. In other words, He was confirming that, because of His miracles, He was indeed the Messiah! This response is key in helping us understand why Christ performed miracles. We can identify the following four main purposes:

1. To announce the arrival of the kingdom of grace in Christ's coming, in accordance with prophecy (see, for example, Isa. 35:3–6)

2. To illustrate Christ's teaching of redemption by grace and the turning back of the consequences of the fall into sin

3. To foreshadow the benefits Christ would accomplish in His work of redemption on the cross

4. To show forth Christ's glory as the Son of God

As we study the miracles, we will see these purposes again and again.

Believing the Miracles

In the past as well as in the present, some have denied that the miracles of the Bible actually took place. If time and space allowed, we could go on at length about some of the arguments people use against miracles and how they can be refuted. Simply put, a person who decides that Christ's miracles couldn't actually have taken place is forcing his or her own view of reality on the Scriptures. Since no one can prove that the miracles did not really happen, this viewpoint is not a statement of fact, but of faith or, rather, unbelief. Such a person is simply saying that he or she does not believe that Christ performed miracles. But once we have eyes to see all that He does in us and around us, instead of doubting Christ's ability, we will experience the joy of seeing countless blessings and miracles that He still performs in our lives. When we focus on His divine presence in our lives, not only will we increase our joy in the Lord but also we will expect more from Him.

The Christ of the Miracles

Is it any wonder that Christ performed miracles when He is such an extraordinary person? He was both perfectly human and perfectly divine. While on earth, He was unique from any other human being.

When we study the miracles, we should never lose sight of the glorious and magnificent Christ who performed them. If you have been brought from darkness to light, He has performed such a miracle in your heart. He has regenerated you, justified you, and reconciled you unto God. These things should astound us no less than the miracles He did when He was on earth.

We should also notice that it is not just divine *power* that shines through Christ's miracles. Divine *attributes* are on display as well—Christ's wisdom, omniscience, love, mercy, and long-suffering are apparent in many of His miracles. What a glimpse they provide of our Lord's character!

Ultimately, all the miracles should lead us to Calvary and the empty tomb, where we see the most miraculous event of all. On the cross and in the empty grave, we see how God brought life and immortality to light in the gospel through the death of a sinless Surety. And so, in each of our studies, we hope to travel the journey from the miracle itself to the cross and the empty tomb. Our focus should not be on the miracles themselves, but on the triune God who purposed and performed them and who applies their truth to the hearts of those who are spiritually blind, lame, leprous, and dead.

Questions

1. Which of Christ's miracles is your favorite? Why do you think it has captured your imagination?

2. There are two extreme views regarding miracles. Some people don't believe in them, while other people want to see them everywhere and believe that they happen today just as they did in the Bible. Think about an appropriate response for both extremes. How can you help people who find the miracles of the Bible difficult to believe or accept?

3. Take another look at the four purposes of the miracles that were given in this chapter. What do they say about God's divinity? What do the miracles in the Bible mean to you personally?

4. Does Satan perform miracles (2 Thess. 2:9)? If so, how are they different from Christ's miracles?

5. Do you see miracles happen in your life? If so, can you name them?

2

The Great Catch of Fish

Luke 5:1–11

When Simon Peter saw it, he fell down at Jesus' knees, saying, Depart from me; for I am a sinful man, O Lord. For he was astonished, and all that were with him, at the draught of the fishes which they had taken.

—LUKE 5:8–9

The miracle of the great catch of fish, recorded in Luke 5, was not the first public miracle Jesus performed. John's gospel records that He had already both supplied wine at the wedding in Cana (2:1–11) and healed a nobleman's son (4:43–54). This miracle would do what those first miracles had done—shed light on Christ's mission on earth, His character and identity, and the calling set before His disciples. Christ would perform a similar miracle later, near the end of His earthly ministry (John 21:1–14), that would also involve a great catch of fish. Obviously, prior to leaving His disciples to go to heaven, Christ wanted to remind them that He was able to do the same miracles that He did early on. And as they obeyed His word, He would fill the nets of the gospel with many sinners whom He would save.

Christ's Word

Simon had already met Christ in Bethabara by Jordan, where John the Baptist had been baptizing (John 1:40–42). His brother, Andrew, had brought and introduced him to Jesus. Some time later, as Luke describes, Jesus found Simon and Andrew fishing and asked to use their boat as He spoke to the people (5:3). This boat was now being used for the fishing of men as Christ taught the multitudes.

After He had finished speaking, Jesus directed Simon to launch forth into the deep for a catch ("draught," Luke 5:4). Simon was an experienced fisherman who had probably been fishing since he was young. Catching the creatures with which God had filled the seas was his livelihood. It is noteworthy that Christ met him as he went about his daily vocation in order to make it training for greater usefulness.

In his transparent way, Simon responded by telling the Lord Jesus that going back out to fish again would be a useless endeavor: "Master, we have toiled all the night, and have taken nothing" (Luke 5:5). However, something made Simon add these words: "Nevertheless at thy word I will let down the net."

This "nevertheless" was the result of the Spirit's work in Simon's life. In this sentence of Simon's we see a very real element in the life of faith, namely, the struggle between our own wisdom (which is foolishness), and the wisdom of Christ, whom Scripture calls "the wisdom of God" (1 Cor. 1:24). Sadly, how often believers call into question the Lord's words; in subtle or more brazen ways we doubt His words to us. We do not obey Him as quickly as Simon did here. And yet a disciple can be characterized as someone who obeys the word of Jesus—despite everything he might see that seems contradictory. Paul explains it like this: "We look not at the things which are seen, but at the things which are not seen" (2 Cor. 4:18). How we need grace to make us more obedient!

This is especially true when we are called to go through situations like "the deep" Simon is directed toward (Luke 5:4). As we go through deep places in life, we lose sight of the bottom and may feel a long way from comfortable, safe ground. We cannot rely on our own strength at times like this; we need to cast ourselves on the Lord and on His word. What a blessing when God's word turns our hearts toward obedience and drives away our doubt and unbelief! We then find, like Simon did, that God's word is best.

Christ's Glory

Compelled by the power of Christ's word, Simon went out into the deep. His net, which had been empty the night before, was now filled with fish to the point that it broke. How did all those fish make it into the net? The powerful voice of the Lord must have gathered them together. After all, Jesus' command to Peter had included an implicit promise: "Launch out into the deep, and let down your nets *for a draught*" (Luke 5:4, emphasis added). The bursting net was His fulfillment of that promise.

When the reality of what had just happened hit Simon, he sank down before Jesus (Luke 5:8). The text explains: "He was astonished…at the draught of the fishes which they had taken" (Luke 5:9). We might say that just as the boat began to sink under the load of fish, "the boat" of Simon's life began to sink under the manifestation of Christ's glory. He was both spiritually and physically overwhelmed by Christ's glory. He realized something that he perhaps had known at some level, but now it overwhelmed him: this was God in his own nature, veiled in flesh, dwelling with him—he who was a sinner. Perhaps he thought with shame of his unbelief just moments ago. How he deserved to be cast away!

Simon wasn't the only one who witnessed Christ's glory in this miracle. The text also mentions James and John, who were with Simon (Luke 5:10). Are you also a witness? Have you joined the countless number of those who have experienced Christ's glory? Have you been astonished by His revelation to you? When the Spirit of God comes, He convinces of sin, and specifically of unbelief (John 16:8–9). We wonder how we could have even uttered a word against the glorious majesty of such a one that charges angels with folly (see Job 4:18). It's no wonder that Simon fell before Christ in humiliation and adoration. Sadly, often we do not see the glory of Christ as we should. What a mercy it is when God takes us into His school and teaches us the knowledge of ourselves by showing us something of Himself and His glory.

Christ's Grace

Before Christ on the ground, Simon could not help himself. He said, "Depart from me; for I am a sinful man" (Luke 5:8). He felt the infinite distance between himself and Christ. He could not see how this majestic One could coexist in the same boat with him, sinful as he was.

Simon's statement was a prayer—an understandable one; nevertheless, it was not the right prayer. Christ mercifully did not answer this prayer. Instead, He bestowed upon Simon grace in a number of ways.

First, Christ showed him *grace by staying with him* rather than departing from him. He could remain with sinful Simon because He had come to take Simon's place under the judgment of God. Already Christ brought forth His grace from Calvary and applied it to Simon in his need.

Second, Christ showed him *grace by comforting him*. He said, "Fear not" (Luke 5:10). Simon had put too much faith in his own wisdom. Then he had despaired of mercy too much. But Christ comforted Simon by settling him and steadying him in His grace.

Third, Christ showed him *grace by commissioning him*. "Fear not; from henceforth thou shalt catch men" (Luke 5:10). Christ was preparing Simon through this experience to look away from his own wisdom and righteousness and instead to lean on the word, glory, and grace of Christ. Probably other fearful occasions would occur when Simon was fishing for men that would overwhelm him. After all, the prophet Isaiah prophesied this back in his day. Using symbolic language, Isaiah spoke of the conversion of many Gentiles as fish being caught in nets: "Then thou shalt see, and flow together, and thine heart shall fear, and be enlarged; because the abundance of the sea shall be converted unto thee, the forces of the Gentiles shall come unto thee" (Isa. 60:5).

Finally, Christ showed him *grace by captivating him*. We read that together with the others, Simon "forsook all, and followed him" (Luke 5:11). This experience had so won him over that he left everything behind and followed Christ at a new level.

Conclusion

Through this miracle, Christ revealed the power of His word, the glory of His person, and the grace in His work. He did something special in the life of Simon to prepare him for the task of being an apostle. However, this is essentially what He does when He draws any sinner to follow Him. He brings us to see our own unworthiness by the light of His great glory. In his commentary on this passage, Calvin writes fittingly: "Thus Christ sinks his own people in the grave, that he may afterwards raise them to life."[2] Indeed, the believer's life is one in which he dies more and more to his own wisdom and ability, and rises again through grace bestowed by this glorious Christ.

Questions

1. Give some instances in the Christian life that are like "the deep" Christ called Peter to launch out into. How should Christ's word help us in such places?

2. What is Christ's implied promise to Peter in Luke 5:4? Discuss its importance and how Peter, in light of it, should have reacted to Christ's word. How should we use the many promises in Scripture?

3. Discuss this statement and how it pertains to Luke 5:1–11: "Christ hears either the prayers His people pray, or the ones they should pray."

4. Perhaps you can relate to the disciples with all their ups and downs. Reflect on Christ's purpose in leading His people through ups and downs.

5. The disciples here literally forsook all. What should Christians forsake that the world keeps? What things might God be calling you to forsake?

3

The Sabbath in Capernaum

Mark 1:21–34

> *And he healed many that were sick of divers diseases, and cast out many devils; and suffered not the devils to speak, because they knew him.*
>
> —MARK 1:34

It was the Sabbath day in Capernaum, the town in which Christ had settled early in His public ministry after facing rejection in His hometown of Nazareth (Matt. 4:13). On this Sabbath day, Christ both preached and performed a number of miracles. He cast out an unclean spirit from a man in the synagogue, cured Peter's mother-in-law of a fever, and healed many others who came to the door of Peter's home that evening. What a Sabbath this must have been! It's no wonder that Christ would later say of Capernaum that it had been "exalted unto heaven" (Matt. 11:23). Certainly, on this Sabbath Christ brought heaven close to Capernaum, and Capernaum close to heaven. Let's look at some of the aspects of this special day.

Heavenly Words

We are not told the specific content of Christ's teaching in the synagogue. But as He had in past sermons, He undoubtedly dealt with themes such as repentance, the kingdom, and divine grace (see Mark 1:15; Luke 4:15–27). Synagogue services at this time usually involved reading prayers, reading Scripture passages, and hearing expositions by scribes. Apparently, the scribes didn't dare go beyond quotations from the fathers, which were opinions from men on various points of doctrine or life. It was all dry and old, lacking freshness and relevance. But Christ's teaching was different. As He spoke, the people quickly recognized two things:

1. *Authority.* Authority refers to the right to speak and act a certain way. For example, kings are given authority, and they in turn may delegate authority to others. Christ had received a commission from the Father to be the chief prophet of His people, and He exercised that commission with authority in His preaching. Christ did not only *speak* about the kingdom; as He spoke, He *showed* the kingdom. People could see the power of the kingdom associated with Christ. There was an authority that they could feel in what Christ said and did.

2. *Freshness.* When the congregants asked, "What new doctrine is this?" they weren't implying that Christ's doctrine was different from the Old Testament teaching they had received. Rather, Christ must have spoken with such authoritative freshness and clarity that His words were unlike any they had ever heard.

Both of these features of Christ's teaching attested that He had come from heaven. His teachings breathed the air of heaven. No wonder they had authority and freshness!

Heavenly Power

Along with Christ's heavenly words in the synagogue came a display of heavenly power. A demon was present in the synagogue that morning. The devil probably didn't mind much when the scribes preached in the synagogue. But when Christ preached, the devil's strongholds were threatened. Suddenly, a loud noise interrupted the service in Capernaum. It was a cry from a man possessed of an unclean spirit. Whenever heaven makes its presence known, hell rushes to do the same. This evil spirit drew attention to itself and away from Jesus Christ.

Some question why this demon would call Christ "the Holy One of God" (Mark 1:24). We should not take this to mean that the demon aligned himself at all with Christ. Instead, we can be sure that the demons do tremble before God and before Christ (James 2:19). Unlike many people, demons know and can recognize holiness for what it is.

The main thing that we see, however, is that wherever the kingdom of God's grace comes, the domain of the devil suffers loss. That is what happens here. Jesus simply rebuked the demon in this man, commanding him to "come out of him," and, crying with a loud voice, the demon came out (Mark 1:25–26). Satan cannot stop the progress of Christ's kingdom. In fact, everything he does will ultimately further God's cause, as it did this Sabbath in Capernaum (see Mark 1:27–28). He is a defeated foe!

Heavenly Compassion

Christ did not show His power only in the public gathering
of His church; that day He also showed His wonderful compassion in private. After the service in the synagogue, Christ
and His disciples went to Simon Peter's house, where they
found his mother-in-law suffering from a fever. We all know
the inconvenience and irritation sickness brings to a house-
hold. This may have been a more dreadful fever than most of
those we are used to, yet it certainly did not rank with things
like demon possession. We might think that Christ would
have saved His miracle-working power for a big problem.

Nevertheless, Christ showed His compassion to Peter's
mother-in-law by standing over her (Luke 4:39), taking her by
the hand (Matt. 8:15), lifting her up (Mark 1:31), and rebuking her fever (Luke 4:39). In an instant, the fever was driven
away, and the woman's strength was renewed. We might have
expected her to continue resting, but instead, "immediately
she arose and ministered unto them" (Luke 4:39). In a single
moment, Christ's miracle turned this home into a place fra-
grant with heaven's bountiful grace.

In fact, the aroma of grace spilled beyond Peter's family
that day. Just a little while later, Capernaum townspeople were
at the door with their sick, dying, and demon-possessed family
members, friends, and neighbors. We read that all throughout the city "all they that had any sick" brought them to Jesus,
"and he laid his hands on every one of them, and healed them"
(Luke 4:40). Did a hospital ever see as many patients healed
in such a short span as that Sabbath evening in Capernaum?
What compassion Christ showed to Capernaum!

A Heavenly Surety

We can be thankful for Sabbaths when heaven seems to come close, when our churches, homes, and communities are impacted by His grace. It's important for us to remember that such blessed Sabbaths come only because of a Surety sent down from heaven. The gospel writer Matthew helps us understand this. After he records some of the events of this Sabbath in Capernaum, he notes how they fulfill a prophecy from the Old Testament: "Himself took our infirmities, and bare our sicknesses" (Matt. 8:17, quoting Isa. 53:4). What an important perspective!

As Christ moved among the sick and the dying that evening, He was not only dispensing healing and turning back the curse, but He was also taking upon Himself these diseases and preparing to die *under* a curse. With this reference to Isaiah's prophecy, Matthew unveils a side to this Sabbath that went largely unnoticed by the people of Capernaum. Christ was bestowing mercies from heaven, but at the cost of His own suffering of hell some three years later.

Equally sobering was that many of Capernaum's people seem not to have profited in any spiritual sense from the events of this day. Only a short time later, Christ mentioned Capernaum by name among those cities that, though "exalted unto heaven" through His ministry, would be "brought down to hell" (Matt. 11:23). May the mercies we have in our churches, homes, and communities not be lost on us! Pray that they would drive us to the feet of this Surety, that we may find true life in Him.

Questions

1. For further study: you can read about this miracle in Matthew 8:14–17 and Luke 4:31–39 also.

2. What can we learn about Christ's speaking with authority? How do we receive a message that makes a claim on us?

3. A fever is something that takes hold of the capacities of the body, keeping them from functioning normally. What sorts of mental, emotional, and spiritual fevers can sometimes take hold of us that we need Christ to rebuke, and how does He do that even today?

4. The devil is still at work and does not avoid the church or our homes. Can you give examples of ways in which he works today? Yet we see that the authority of Christ is enough to silence him. How can we fight against attacks from the devil?

5. Peter's mother-in-law used her newfound strength in the service of the Lord. Think of a time when God blessed or healed you. How can you show Him your gratitude for this?

6. Peter's mother-in-law served Christ in the confines of the house. How can you serve God concretely in your place of influence?

4

The Cleansing of the Leper

Luke 5:12–15

And it came to pass, when [Jesus] was in a certain city, behold a man full of leprosy: who seeing Jesus fell on his face, and besought him, saying, Lord, if thou wilt, thou canst make me clean.
—LUKE 5:12

As we saw in chapter 1, Christ's miracles were intended for various purposes, one of which was to illustrate the gospel message. Whether He was driving out a demon, healing someone who was diseased, or raising someone from the dead, the Lord proved each time that He had come to deal with the curse that was the result of sin. The miracle performed upon the leper in Luke 5 pictures for us in an especially clear way what Christ does when He cleanses us from our sins.

Throughout the Old Testament, the Lord made clear that leprosy was a picture of sin and its effects. The prophet Isaiah used the picture of a leper to describe the spiritual state of Israel: "From the sole of the foot even unto the head there is no soundness in it; but wounds, and bruises, and putrefying sores" (Isa. 1:6). The comparison was highly appropriate. Leprosy was a terrible disease that rendered a person unclean. Lepers could not enter into the company of people or into holy places such as the temple or synagogues. They were shunned and avoided by people. The leper would waste away physically until he would become unrecognizable, and then finally die.

The ceremonial laws dealt rigorously with any potential leprosy. There was undoubtedly a medical reason for this, for the laws helped prevent the spread of this contagious disease throughout the society of Israel. However, the detail, dread, and decisiveness with which the priests treated leprosy (Lev. 13–14) were certainly telling. Offerings of atonement had to take place as well as an elaborate ritual of cleansing (Lev. 14:1–32). The legislation concerning leprosy ends ominously: "This is the law of him in whom is the plague of leprosy, whose hand is not able to get that which pertaineth to his cleansing" (Lev. 14:32).

There was no known cure for leprosy as we see, for example, in the cases of Miriam (Num. 12:10–15) and Naaman (2 Kings 5). Any cure was a result only of God's miraculous intervention. A miracle needed to take place, and in this passage in Luke we see such a miracle. In fact, we see three miracles that comprise the miracle of the cleansing of the leper.

Miracle 1: The Leper Came to Jesus

We don't know how this leper heard of Jesus, but the gospel of Mark tells us that Jesus' "fame spread abroad throughout all the region round about Galilee" (Mark 1:28). Perhaps a relative or friend of this leper came near the area where he lived and called out, "We believe Messiah has come. It's Jesus of Nazareth. He may be your only hope!"

What is more remarkable, though, is that the leper not only heard of Jesus but also came to believe that Christ could heal him. Though Christ had previously cast out demons and healed many from various diseases, there was not yet any record of Christ healing someone from leprosy. It is not likely that any lepers would have been part of those He had healed on the Sabbath evening in Capernaum, for those who were healed came from the city (Mark 1:33–34), and no leper would have been allowed there.

Had someone perhaps told the leper about the sermon Christ had preached in Nazareth, when He had made clear that He had been anointed to "heal the brokenhearted" (Luke 4:18)? Certainly, this man's heart had broken beneath the stroke of leprosy. If he knew the words of Psalm 38, he found them applicable: "I am troubled; I am bowed down greatly; I go mourning all the day long. For my loins are filled with a loathsome disease: and there is no soundness in my flesh. I am feeble and sore broken: I have roared by reason of the disquietness of my heart" (vv. 6–8).

Could word have reached this leper that in the sermon in Luke 4 Christ had referred to "Naaman the Syrian," the pagan leper who had been cleansed (v. 27)? Whatever the means, it is clear that the Lord of heaven was drawing this leper to His Son (John 6:44). He had worked in him faith that was firmly persuaded that Christ was indeed the Son of God, "able...to save...to the uttermost" (Heb. 7:25), even a leper like himself. After all, since this Jesus was the Son of God, not even leprosy would be too strong for Him. Of the Lord alone is it said "who healeth all thy diseases; who redeemeth thy life from destruction" (Ps. 103:3–4).

And so one day this man, whose leprosy was very advanced (Luke 5:12 calls him "a man full of leprosy"), left his area of quarantine. In spite of the odds against him and the obstacles facing him, he made his way toward Jesus. At this moment, Jesus was "in a certain city" (Luke 5:12), surrounded by "great multitudes" (Matt. 8:1). How the crowds would have looked at the leper in horror as he approached the Lord! And yet, nothing could make this man turn back.

Miracle 2: Jesus Touched the Leper

The crowds may have drawn back as the leper approached, but Jesus did not. The Great Physician had not come to save the healthy, but the sick (Mark 2:17). Christ remained there as this leper knelt down (Mark 1:40), "fell on his face" (Luke 5:12), and "worshipped him" (Matt. 8:2). He hurled all that was left of himself—a leprous bundle of corruption—before the holy Son of God. Scarcely have two more opposites ever met: he wretched, and Christ, the worthy One; he foul, and Christ, the fountain; he powerless, and Christ, all power.

There is no doubt from this man's words and actions that he understood the exalted character of Christ. But this exalted view did not keep him from the Savior; instead, it drew him to the only One great enough to deal with his desperate case. Sometimes people think that Christ is too great to deal with them. The Word of God teaches us the opposite through this leper's story. Because of his extreme situation, the leper needed a great Savior, and none less than the Son of God would do. In fact, notice his confession: "Thou canst make me clean" (Luke 5:12).

It is important to notice that this man spoke not of healing, but of *cleansing*. What plagued him most about this disease was that it made him unclean before God and man. Unlike what many other lepers would have wanted, this leper didn't just want his body, his life, or his future back. Like David, his chief concern was this: "Purge me with hyssop, and I shall be clean: wash me, and I shall be whiter than snow" (Ps. 51:7).

But notice also that though he was firmly persuaded of Christ's ability, there was still some doubt in his mind about Christ's willingness to cleanse him. What he says makes this clear: "*If thou wilt*, thou canst make me clean" (Luke 5:12, emphasis added). This man portrays for us what countless people think, feel, and say when they are coming to Christ: they are convinced in their hearts of Christ's ability, yet they doubt and fear whether Christ is willing to cleanse them, personally and specifically. How many of us share this man's doubts! Often our shame for sin and the realization that we do not deserve to be cleansed and forgiven by God hide from our view the willingness of the Lord that He so frequently and tenderly conveys in His promises (e.g., Isa. 1:18; Jer. 3:12–13).

But the important thing is that this man's doubts and fears did not keep him away from the Lord. His need and desire were stronger than his fears and doubts. He *must* have this Savior's cleansing. You can almost hear his thoughts: "I cannot wait any longer. I am full of leprosy. I may not have much longer. How do I know that this Savior will still be here tomorrow? What if my delay turns into regret? If He is not willing, He will have to tell me so Himself, while I lay at

His feet. I don't stand a chance without Him anyway. I must go, today, while I still can." And so he came.

The second miracle of this passage is that Christ did not shrink away from the polluted heap in front of Him. Instead, He "put forth his hand, and touched him" (Luke 5:13). The priests of the Old Testament would never touch anyone who was unclean (see Hag. 2:11–13), but this High Priest can still "be touched with the feeling of our infirmities" (Heb. 4:15). To His touch, the Savior added precious words: "I will: be thou clean" (Luke 5:13). The Lord drove away any doubt about His willingness: "I will," He said. He is mercy in the flesh, and no sinner who comes kneeling at His feet pleading for cleansing will be turned away.

Miracle 3: Jesus Cleansed the Leper

"And immediately the leprosy departed from him" (Luke 5:13). Christ had shown His willingness by touching the leper; now He proved His power by cleansing the leper. The picture we get is of the leprosy leaving the man immediately, dramatically, and decisively, driven away by the almighty power of the Savior. The horrible disease that had brought him almost to the brink of death was now powerless. From the top of his head to the soles of his feet, the disease vanished and wholeness returned. The leper had been thoroughly and completely cleansed.

Christ then commanded the man to show himself to the temple priest (Luke 5:14), as Moses had specified in the law (see Lev. 14). This was proof that Christ had come not to destroy the law, but to fulfill it (Matt. 5:17–20). Isaiah had prophesied that Christ would "magnify the law, and make it honourable" (Isa. 42:21). Christ wanted the sons of Aaron to know that the cleanser of lepers had appeared on the scene. The Lord didn't unravel the Mosaic ceremonies at this point. Priestly ceremonies would be fulfilled as He shed His blood on the cross. Soon He would be "cut off out of the land of the living"; for the transgression of his people he would be stricken (Isa. 53:8). Until then, there was still the need for animal blood to be shed.

Although the blood of animals would need to be shed until those ceremonies were fulfilled at Calvary, the priests were being forewarned by this leper's showing himself to them that they would soon be out of a job. We don't know whether the leper went to the priests as Jesus directed him to, but we do know that he did not obey Jesus' other direction—"tell no man" (Luke 5:14). Instead, the leper began to spread the news of his cure far abroad. Before we blame the leper too much, we should examine our own hearts to see whether we always render exact obedience to Christ's commands in His Word. And consider this: too often we commit the opposite offense. While this man was too outspoken, we are often too silent about what God has done for us. Where Christ's cleansing power is at work, His renewing power will also prevail until those who have been cleansed from sin will forever testify of His power, glory, and grace.

Questions

1. For further study: you can read about this miracle in Matthew 8:1–4 and Mark 1:40–45 also.

2. Describe some of the ways the plague of leprosy
pictures the plague of our hearts.

3. What people in society do we look down upon?
How would the Lord Jesus have dealt with them,
and what does this teach us?

4. Matthew records this miracle after Jesus' giving
the Sermon on the Mount (see 8:1–4). Most students of the Bible think Matthew does that to
show the power of Christ not only to teach the
law but also to cleanse those who are defiled with
respect to the law. Read Romans 8:2–4 and discuss how Paul makes that same point.

5. How would this story have been different if the
leper had doubted Christ's ability instead of His
willingness? In other words, what would have
been the problem if he had said, "If thou canst,
thou wilt make me clean"?

6. Christ brought this leper into the community
again while He was forced soon after to withdraw
to desert places (see Mark 1:45). What does this
say about the heart of God?

7. Do we share the great things that God has done
in our lives? Why, or why not? If we shared, how
would this change the world around us?

5

The Healing of the Paralytic

Luke 5:15–26

When Jesus perceived their thoughts, he answering said unto them, What reason ye in your hearts? Whether is easier, to say, Thy sins be forgiven thee; or to say, Rise up and walk?
—LUKE 5:22–23

If the cleansing of the leper demonstrated what Christ can do with the pollution of sin, the miracle we will consider next shows what God can do with the inability that plagues us because of our sin. Sin so disables us that, without a mighty work of grace upon us, we are unable to come to Christ for cleansing. This miracle teaches us that even when sinners have no power, Christ has "power on earth to forgive sins" (Matt. 9:6; Mark 2:10). Let's trace this out by looking at six aspects of the miracle.

Power

Christ was teaching in a house in Capernaum. Many had gathered to hear Him—so many that the house was full and people were pressing in around the door. Though both Matthew (9:1–8) and Mark (2:1–13) record this incident, only the evangelist Luke, in chapter 5, mentions an interesting detail about what else was present that day: "the power of the Lord was present to heal them" (v. 17). Just before this, in verse 16, we are told that Christ had been praying in the wilderness, so *power* came after *prayer*. The histories of nations, churches, and individuals often record times of power that came after special seasons of prayer. Though Christ began by teaching, healing would also happen in this house.

Powerlessness

Luke 5:18 tells us that "men brought in a bed a man which was taken with a palsy…to lay him before [Jesus]." "Taken with a palsy" means paralyzed, likely from the waist down. This man could neither stand nor walk. What a picture of all of us on a spiritual level! We were made to walk with God, but because of our sins we can neither stand nor walk before Him as we ought.

Despite his miserable condition, this paralytic man was greatly blessed—he had four friends who cared for him (Luke 5:18). How wonderful it is to have even one true friend! We don't know much about these friends, but we do know that all five of the men had one thing in common—faith (Luke 5:20). The Holy Spirit had worked in these men the persuasion that Christ was able to help them.

But there were obstacles for them. The crowd at the house where Christ was that day prevented their access to Him. Would the men turn away and give up on their hope of a cure for their friend? Many do turn away from following Christ when obstacles present themselves. But, as we'll see, the true faith in these men's hearts shows itself in their persistence.

Persistence

Houses in Israel at that time often had an exterior staircase that led to a flat roof. And so these men, unable to get through the door, instead made their way up the stairs to the roof (Luke 5:19). The people in the house likely heard the noise of their feet on the stairs, and the four men probably strained to hear where Christ's voice was coming from in order to know where to open up the roof. In those days, roofs were made of rough rafters covered with branches or tiles plastered together with a mud-like substance. It might not have been difficult to break a section of the roof apart, but it was certainly an unusual thing to do! It would have been messy as well. Imagine pieces of baked mud falling around Christ as He was teaching the people. Yet this is evidence that true faith is not easily intimidated. In a sermon on this passage, Spurgeon observed: "When four true hearts are set upon the spiritual good of a sinner, their holy hunger will break through stone walls or house roofs."[3]

The friends kept up their efforts until the paralytic man was let down "before Jesus" (Luke 5:19). What a beautiful phrase! True faith always runs until it comes "before Jesus." Like iron moving toward a magnet, so faith moves toward Christ until it clings to Him. Faith does not have this power in itself, but it is driven by need. Ultimately, it wasn't some power or virtue in faith that saved this man; instead, *Christ* saved him by faith. The Spirit of God drove the faith of these five men until they came with all their powerlessness to the only powerful One.

Pardon

What a remarkable picture the Scripture paints in Luke 5:19: a *powerless* sinner in front of a *powerful* Savior. Remember how Luke noted that there was power present to heal (5:17). Now, finally, here was someone in desperate need of healing! But physical healing was not the first priority for Christ. He saw beyond this man's misery to its root cause, and He addressed that cause before He addressed its effect. We can be thankful when the Lord teaches us our real problems. "Man, thy sins are forgiven thee" (Luke 5:20), Christ declares. Notice the following about the pardon Christ issued to the paralytic:

- It was *authoritative* pardon. His words and tone evidenced this authority, but Christ also demonstrated that authority, as we will see (see Luke 5:24).

- It was *substitutionary* pardon. He could issue this pardon because He would die for this man's sin on the cross.

- It was *defended* pardon. The Pharisees would immediately dispute this pardon (Luke 5:21). This must have unnerved the man who had been pardoned. These doctors of the law were disputing what Christ had just said. Can't you imagine the paralytic asking, "Who is right?" Yet Christ took the side of the pardoned sinner, shielding him against this devilish attack. He defended the pardon by pointing to Himself, and proved it by the actual healing.

Proof

Christ not only perceived the faith of the five men before Him; He could also see into the hearts of the Pharisees: "Jesus perceived their thoughts" (Luke 5:22). The Pharisees were offended that Christ would forgive this man his sins. What enmity even religious men can have against free grace! In this, the enmity targeted the Savior Himself. Nevertheless, by healing the man, Christ proved that He had power to forgive this man his sins.

How eminently Christ would soon prove again that He had power to forgive sin when He would die for sinners on the cross, pay their debt, and rise again. He would prove it again in His ascension and at Pentecost. And now He proves it over again in the gospel when He delivers sinners from their sins.

Sadly, many are content to examine the power instead of experiencing it. Many are content to observe rather than obey. Notice Luke's mention that "there were Pharisees and doctors of the law sitting by" (Luke 5:17). The implication is that these men were content to be religious onlookers. Such people always exist, but they never feel their spiritual paralysis. Others, however, feel their sin and perhaps wonder if God can forgive them. Christ proved here that He has power on earth to forgive sins. How many of us are only looking on, spiritually speaking, while we never feel our own spiritual need and paralysis. What a blessing it is when we are made to feel our need! If you do know your need, learn from this miracle that Christ has power on earth to forgive sins. Do not be turned back by obstacles. Do not rest until you come to His feet.

Praise

When the Son of Man forgives and heals, there will be praise! The man who had been forgiven and healed rose up before the crowd, took up his stretcher, and departed, glorifying God. Others couldn't help but join this man in praising. They too "glorified God, and were filled with fear, saying, We have seen strange things to day" (Luke 5:26).

A true experience of God's forgiving grace always leads to praising God. We will call on others to come and hear what God has done for our souls. We will say with the psalmist, "Come and hear, all ye that fear God, and I will declare what he hath done for my soul. I cried unto him with my mouth, and he was extolled with my tongue" (Ps. 66:16–17).

Questions

1. For further study: you can read about this miracle in Matthew 9:1–8 and Mark 2:1–12 also.

2. Christ's miracle in Luke 5 proved something about Himself and what He had come to do (v. 24). What point can we draw from this regarding the other miracles Christ performed?

3. A recurring promise in the Old Testament was that God would come and pardon His people's sins. See, for example, Isaiah 43:25; Jeremiah 31:34; and Micah 7:18–20. Is Christ teaching us here that we should look only for the miracle of the cleansing of our souls?

4. How can we be used like these four friends to bring others to Christ? Where might we look for people like this paralytic?

5. What lesson do you take from Christ's gladly bearing the disturbance and mess caused by these five men for the sake of having a needy sinner come to His feet? Think of a time you look back on that the Lord bore with a lot of "disturbance" from you. What does this say about Him?

6. How could the Pharisees seem to be so concerned with the honor of God and yet so wrong (Luke 5:21)? What lesson does this teach us?

7. What obstacles do you find in your way to Christ? How can you deal with these obstacles in light of this passage?

6

The Healing of the Centurion's Servant

Matthew 8:5–13

The centurion answered and said, Lord, I am not worthy that thou shouldest come under my roof: but speak the word only, and my servant shall be healed.
—MATTHEW 8:8

Our world sees greatness as having power, prestige, or possessions. In the kingdom of God, however, the greatest is the least, and the last is first. Christ had taught this principle in the Sermon on the Mount, the great charter of the kingdom of heaven (Matt. 5:3). Shortly after He finished this sermon, we meet a man who embodied this greatness. As a centurion, this Gentile man was considered great by the world. But his true greatness was not at all related to the things the world admires. The Lord called his *faith* great (Matt. 8:10). Thus, the real miracle of this story is not even the healing of his servant, but the faith that comes into evidence in and around this miracle.

A Great Need

In the Sermon on the Mount, Christ taught that we should seek, ask, and knock (Matt. 7:7–8). We don't know whether the centurion of this passage had been present and heard these words, but he certainly did take his need to Christ. He was in great need because his servant (literally, his slave) was deathly ill. This illness had such a hold that it was both paralyzing the sick man and sending him into convulsions (Matt. 8:6). Luke notes that he "was ready to die" (7:2). This verse also tells us that the centurion cared deeply for his slave, which is remarkable, for at that time slaves were commonly considered to be property. Also touching is this concern and love for human life from a military officer who was used to violence and death. Many like him would have thought little of replacing one slave with another.

The centurion's track record was notable not just because of his real regard for another human, but also for another reason. According to the elders of the Jews, he loved the Jewish nation and had even personally financed the construction of a synagogue (Luke 7:5). This would have made the headlines because the Jewish land was occupied by the Romans at that time, who were generally viewed as oppressive enemies. The centurion was stationed in Capernaum as a representative of the Roman government and was to enforce its policies. How remarkable that these elders say that this man loved the Jewish nation! Certainly he must have been an exception among the many centurions stationed throughout Israel.

Matthew seems to imply that the centurion himself came to Jesus. Luke fills in the picture by mentioning that the centurion sent some of the Jewish elders. Elders were representatives of the nation. It is remarkable that these elders came so willingly on his behalf. Their coming at the centurion's behest shows clearly that he had gained the love of many.

We can understand, then, why the Jewish elders would bring this to Christ's attention. Notice how these Jewish elders ask for Christ's help based on their judgment that the centurion "was worthy" (Luke 7:4). This requires some scrutiny. Can anyone be *worthy* so that Christ must answer his prayers? Can anyone *deserve* to have his problems remedied? Will any of us ever *deserve* Christ driving away sickness and death because of something we do or some church we have built?

But before we criticize the Jewish elders for reasoning this way, let's examine how we might think, talk, and pray in similar terms: "Lord, I have been working so hard for Thee. Why is this trouble in my life?" Or, "Lord, he has done so much good in Thy cause or in our nation. Certainly, Thou wilt hear us when we ask this for this man." This kind of reasoning comes straight out of the covenant of works, the principle to which we gravitate. Even God's people can lapse into thinking in terms of a covenant of works. We can definitely infer, however, that the centurion did not think of himself as worthy. Matthew and Luke use the words "beseeching" and "entreating" to describe his request of Jesus (Matt. 8:5; Luke 7:4). He was driven by his need and by what he had "heard of Jesus" (Luke 7:3).

Christ had made Capernaum the base of His Galilean ministry, so many of His miracles occurred there (Luke 4:31–44). For example, He had driven a demon out of a possessed man, perhaps in the very synagogue the centurion had financed (Mark 1:25). He cured Peter's mother-in-law of a fever (Mark 1:31), and later that same evening he had "healed many that were sick of divers diseases, and cast out many devils" (Mark 1:34). He had healed the paralytic after having forgiven his sins (Mark 2:10–12). He had cleansed a leper somewhere in the vicinity, and the reports of it had spread through the whole area (Mark 1:45). He had also spoken with authority in the synagogues, and, in the Sermon on the Mount, he had unfolded the kingdom of heaven and Himself as its king (Matt. 5–7; Luke 6). He had urged His hearers to strive to enter into the gate to the kingdom of heaven (Matt. 7:13). Some or all of these things had an effect on this centurion. Many others considered Jesus a great miracle worker, and from the way this passage begins, one might at first imagine that this is how the centurion thought of Him as well. However, it quickly became clear that the reports of Jesus had had a far more profound effect on him.

A Great King

Even though the Jewish elders made their request on a misguided basis, we read, "Then Jesus went with them" (Luke 7:6). As He approached the house, word must have reached the centurion that the Lord was on His way. The man sent another delegation, this time made up of his friends. These friends said something very different and came with this message: "Lord, trouble not thyself: for I am not worthy" (Luke 7:6). The elders said he *was* worthy; he said he was *not* worthy. Why did he say that?

This fits with our earlier point. Please understand that the man did not suddenly change his mind. He knew all along he was unworthy. That is why he had sent others to Christ and did not come himself: "Wherefore neither thought I myself worthy to come unto thee" (Luke 7:7). Clearly, he realized that the distance between the Lord and himself was not traversable. He needed others to mediate for him, and when it looked as if the Lord was about to come under the same roof with him, he had to make clear that he understood his absolute unworthiness.

This man must have understood something of Christ's divine character. What he had heard about Christ must have convinced him that He was a divine king with authority over all things, both seen and unseen. The centurion might have one hundred men he could tell to go or come, but Christ rules over all. He was a centurion representing Rome—but this Jesus was a representative of heaven and the kingdom of God, with authority over all. Hadn't one word from Christ's mouth been enough to cure from disease, banish demons, and forgive sins? This centurion had learned to ascribe all power in heaven and earth to Jesus Christ. He must have felt something of what John Newton felt when he wrote:

> Thou art coming to a King,
> Large petitions with thee bring;
> For His grace and pow'r are such,
> None can ever ask too much.[4]

Along with this centurion's view of Christ came his understanding of himself. He realized that he was not equal to Christ. In essence, this centurion put the crown on the head of Christ, whose right it is to wear it (Ezek. 21:27). Frequently in the Scriptures we read about people who were made aware of God's greatness and their smallness. Abraham said he was "dust and ashes" compared to the Lord (Gen. 18:27). John the Baptist said he was not worthy to unloose the latchet of Christ's shoes (John 1:27). The prodigal said to his father, "I am not 'worthy to be called thy son'" (Luke 15:19). This was the centurion's experience. He knew he was not worthy of Christ's help. This knowledge of God and of self is the fruit of God's work in our hearts, for we don't reach this conclusion by ourselves. He makes us sense His worthiness and our unworthiness. Note that the centurion expressed this feeling most directly and forcefully as Christ was coming toward him. The closer Christ comes, the more unworthy we feel. Isn't that true?

A Great Faith

What did the centurion display? Christ gave it a name: "great faith" (Matt. 8:10). Many people think so differently. They imagine that great faith shows itself as the elders did—it steps up to Christ and assumes man's greatness and worthiness. Many think that if they put up a big church building and parking lot, the Lord will surely bless them for their liberality and vision, and they pray like that. But "great faith" does the opposite: "I am not worthy...but speak the word only" (Matt. 8:8).

According to Luke, the centurion instructed his friends to say to Jesus, "Trouble not thyself...but say in a word" (Luke 7:7). One word from Christ was enough. The centurion didn't prescribe to Christ how it should all go—how, when, and where this miracle should take place. Great faith is content to leave it all to Christ and His word.

Questions

1. For further study: you can read about this miracle in Luke 7:1–10 also.

2. The Bible tells us that Christ marveled twice: once at the unbelief of the Nazarenes (Mark 6:6), and once at the faith of this centurion (Matt. 8:10). What does it mean that the Son of God marveled? What significance is there that we read nowhere of Christ marveling at the things we often marvel at, but instead at the *faith* of one person and the *unbelief* of others?

3. The elders assumed the centurion deserved Jesus' time and attention because of the good deeds he had performed. How do we show the same attitude as the elders in this passage in our prayers and in our general view of how this world operates? How can we get rid of this "entitlement" attitude?

4. Read Proverbs 22:1 and the first part of Ecclesiastes 7:1 and discuss how we see this operating in the centurion. How do these verses apply to how you should see yourself before God and others?

5. How does the Holy Spirit work a true sense of unworthiness? Is there such a thing as a false sense of unworthiness that has nothing to do with godliness? What is the difference?

6. Read the first part of 2 Thessalonians 1:3. If we are believers, how might we seek for and register growth in faith?

7

The Miracle at the Gate of Nain

Luke 7:11–17

> *[Jesus] said, Young man, I say unto thee, Arise. And he that was dead sat up, and began to speak. And he delivered him to his mother. And there came a fear on all.*
>
> —LUKE 7:14–16

The city of Nain lay at the eastern edge of the beautiful valley of Jezreel. Three miles to the north of the city was tree-covered Mount Tabor, and farther in the distance was snow-capped Mount Hermon. Christ had been in the city of Capernaum, some twenty-five miles away from Nain. But on this particular day, He approached Nain on an errand of mercy.

A Stark Contrast

Before Christ arrived in Nain, however, another visitor, death, had already come and showed its power. The effects of this power were visible in a funeral procession making its way out of the city. Luke poignantly depicts two crowds meeting just outside the gate of Nain. As Christ was approaching the city followed by "much people," disciples as well as curious onlookers (Luke 7:11), the funeral procession was leaving, on its way to a graveyard outside the city (Luke 7:12). What a contrast between the two groups! Those leaving the city were filled with grief and sorrow. Those coming toward the city were filled with excitement. A company of death, you could say, encountered a company of life.

At the head of the funeral procession, men with somber faces carried a bier, a board with narrow sides. On this bier lay the body of a young man. Beside the bier walked the young man's mother. This was not the first time this woman had been part of a funeral procession for a loved one. Luke tells us that she "was a widow" (7:12). How she must have leaned on this only son after her husband's death! Yet death, the king of terrors, had struck again, snuffing out the son's life as well. Never again would she hear him coming in the door, home again after working all day to provide a livelihood for both of them. Never again would she enjoy reminiscing with him about his father at the dinner table. This boy was cut off early in life.

Christ had created this world without graveyards. But because of sin, death now reigns over all our world (Rom. 5:14). It takes away the old, but it can also take the young. What emptiness, loneliness, and grief it causes. Perhaps inwardly this woman was thinking what the psalmist expressed: "I will say unto God my rock, Why hast thou forgotten me? why go I mourning because of the oppression of the enemy?" (Ps. 42:9).

However, this woman would find that God had not forgotten her. She was anticipating a day of mourning, but things would turn out very differently. The Son of God, who had come to meet her just outside the city, would show His mercy and power in her life in an unforgettable way.

A Remarkable Command

In Luke 7:13 we read moving words: "And when the Lord saw her, he had compassion on her, and said unto her, Weep not." Absorbed in her grief, this woman may not have even noticed the approach of Christ. But He came to meet her in her need with His word. There are three ways in which this verse foreshadows, or anticipates, what is about to happen.

1. *It refers to Christ as "Lord."* Luke is drawing attention to the power of Christ by using this title. Peter had confessed Jesus as Lord (5:8); the leper had confessed Him as Lord (5:12); and the centurion with the sick servant had confessed Him as "Lord" (7:6). Now this widow would come to know him as the Lord of life and death.

2. *It highlights Christ's compassion.* Christ was not only proving Himself to be a powerful king but also to be a compassionate high priest, who could be touched with the feeling of this widow's infirmity (see Heb. 4:15). He did not turn away from this sad procession, content to revel in the attention people were giving Him. When He saw the sorrow of this widow, His heart was touched by the misery that sin had brought into this world. (In heaven, His heart is still the same toward needy and miserable sinners today.)

3. *It includes an amazing command.* Before Christ even performed the miracle, He called this widow to live in the light of it. "Weep not," He told her (Luke 7:13). This is a remarkable word from the

Lord Jesus. This woman had every reason to weep, and yet He told her not to. Essentially, He was calling this woman to exercise faith in Him as the resurrection and the life. This is similar to what He calls His people to do today. It is not that we may not weep when our family and friends die. Even Christ wept at Lazarus's grave (John 11:35). However, when believers' loved ones die in the Lord, they are taught not to weep as those who have no hope (1 Thess. 4:13). The resurrection gospel needs to impinge upon all of our lives. This is what the Lord wanted the woman to know even before He performed a miracle in her presence—the resurrection joy that comes when we see His resurrection power at work. The day is coming when God will "wipe away all tears" from the eyes of His children (Rev. 21:4).

A Glorious Conqueror

Luke 7:14 reads so majestically: "He came and touched the bier: and they that bare him stood still. And he said, Young man, I say unto thee, Arise." It's interesting to notice that in the original language of this passage, Christ spoke only six words—two to the mother, and four to the young man. The most important of the words was the last one: "Arise." This single word was loaded with meaning. Each time Christ raised someone from the dead, whether it was Jairus's daughter, Lazarus, or this young man, He spoke, as one commentator says, with a "powerful brevity."

Notice also that Christ raised the young man by speaking to him. To the skeptical onlooker, it may have seemed ridiculous that Christ would address someone who was dead. A dead person can neither hear nor obey a command. But not even death can keep someone from hearing the Lord's voice! As John 5:25 says, "The dead shall hear the voice of the Son of God: and they that hear shall live."

Christ didn't draw back from the bier on which the young man lay. He who was the Holy One of Israel could not be rendered unclean by touching the bier. Instead, death was forced to retreat in the face of the One who would hold the keys of death and hell through His death and resurrection (Rev. 1:18).

Thus this widow discovered that she could safely trust in Him who is the Lord of the widows (Jer. 49:11). Christ added to the miracle this tender touch: "He delivered him to his mother" (Luke 7:15). He scooped the young man up in His arms and gave him to his mother again. The boy had been a gift from the Lord when she had received him at his birth. Now she received him a second time, as evidence of the Savior's power and compassion.

We read: "And he that was dead...began to speak" (Luke 7:15). We can only wonder what this young man said! Certainly the conversations that followed were filled with words of rejoicing and wonder. The day that had begun with such misery and sadness turned into such gladness and rejoicing. That's what Christ's grace and power do!

Luke 7:17 tells us that the news of Christ's death-defeating power reached people far and wide. One of those people was John the Baptist, who was imprisoned in the dungeon of Herod (see Luke 7:18–19). Somehow through God's providence, news of this miracle reached John's prison cell.

He would soon lose his life through the cruelty of Herodias and the cowardice of Herod. What a comfort it must have been for John to hear the tidings of Him who was the resurrection and the life!

Many others heard the reports of this miracle as well. The whole of this valley region was abuzz with glad news that "God hath visited his people" (Luke 7:16). What a fulfillment of what Psalm 89:12 says about the mountains of this region: "Tabor and Hermon shall rejoice in thy name."

A few years later, Mount Calvary and the Mount of Olives witnessed a far greater miracle near the gate of another city. Just outside of Jerusalem, death retreated from this ultimate Conqueror. Not a word was spoken; He who was the Word arose with the power of an endless life (Heb. 7:16). And now to all our earth, so filled with death and sorrow, this Prince of Life speaks His word, and death must relinquish its prey (John 5:24). Christ has "brought life and immortality to light through the gospel" (2 Tim. 1:10).

Questions

1. Read 2 Corinthians 1:4–5 and compare it to Luke 7:11–17. What can we see of the character of Christ here? What can this mean for our lives?

2. Christ used this child's death for a higher purpose. What purpose was this? Have you gone through circumstances in which—looking back—the hand of God was visible through everything?

3. What was the reaction of the crowd to this miracle? Have you ever witnessed God's miracle in your or someone else's life? How did you react to it? Why is our response to God's work so important?

4. How does this miracle point to the death of Christ? What does this tell us about the power of God over life and death? Does this comfort you?

5. When Christ told the woman to "weep not," He offered her a promise in her grief. What promises from the Bible does Christ give us when we grieve? How might this comfort the Lord's people when they feel unable to pray at times?

6. What does Christ's compassion tell us about His care for hurting people? How can we bring His comfort to hurting people around us? Give a practical example.

7. What parallels are there between the boy's physical resurrection and spiritual resurrection?

8

Silencing the Storm at Sea

Mark 4:35–41

And they feared exceedingly, and said one to another, What manner of man is this, that even the wind and the sea obey him?
—MARK 4:41

It can be relatively easy to restore calm in certain situations. A skilled teacher can calm a rambunctious class. A mother can often calm a restless child. A doctor can calm an anxious patient with the good news of a favorable medical report. With skill, these situations can be managed. But there are other situations in which bringing calm is beyond us. If you stand next to an ocean during a storm, your words will do nothing to stop the raging of the sea. Waves and wind just won't obey you, and neither do some other kinds of "winds and waves." Think of the winds of anger and bitterness that form from the conflicts between individuals or nations. Think of the wave of heartache that crashes over you when you lose a loved one. Think of the hidden storms in our hearts—of doubt, of guilt, and of anxious thoughts. It is beyond us to calm troubled consciences or to reach into despairing hearts. We need the One whose miraculous power the disciples witnessed during a storm on the Sea of Galilee.

Mysterious Classroom

It had been a busy day for the Lord Jesus and His disciples. For most of the day, He had preached to the multitudes. It was the first time He had preached using parables, earthly stories with heavenly meanings, such as the parable of the sower, the parable of the grain of mustard seed, and the parable of leaven. It must have been a mysterious day as well. These parables' meanings about the kingdom of God were hidden in a way and could not be easily grasped. Afterward, Jesus had spent time with only His disciples and explained to them the meaning of what He had taught.

The mysterious day was to become a mysterious night. Someone once said that during the day Jesus had His disciples in the classroom; during the night He would give them a practicum.

So in the evening Jesus said, "Let us pass over unto the other side" (Mark 4:35). They were by the Sea of Galilee, also known as the Sea of Genesereth or the Sea of Tiberias. This lake was some fifteen miles long by eight miles wide, surrounded on most sides by hills and mountains. Because many of the disciples were fishermen, they had traveled this sea frequently. We can safely assume that they entered the ship oblivious to any sign of danger. After all, this was their Lord's order. Matthew states rather matter-of-factly: "He gave commandment to depart unto the other side" (8:18).

As they set sail, we're told, Jesus went down into the stern of the boat and fell asleep. What proof this was that Jesus was truly and fully man! After all, He had been teaching the multitudes all day; after a rigorous day of work, a good sleep is a gift. It is interesting to note that just a few hours before, Christ had mentioned sleep: "So is the kingdom of God, as if a man should cast seed into the ground; and should sleep, and rise night and day, and the seed should spring and grow up" (Mark 4:26–27). Now that Jesus had spent the day sowing the seed of God's word, He, like the farmer in that parable, could sleep. God's purpose with the seed would be accomplished. Psalm 127:2 says that it is vain to stay up late and deprive the body of sleep: "He giveth his beloved sleep." In the stern of the boat, God the Father was giving His beloved Son rest and sleep after a full day of work.

Desperate Disciples

While Jesus was resting in the stern of the boat, the sea underneath grew restless: "There arose a great storm of wind" (Mark 4:37). Although this lake is usually calm, the wind coming over the surrounding mountains can suddenly raise a vehement storm. A squall threw the sea into such tossing and turning that we read that the "waves beat into the ship" until "it was now full" (Mark 4:37). Imagine trying to maintain your stand on deck as waves rapidly fill your boat with water.

What can you do when the ship of your life is full? One more wave, and the ship will sink down. You've bailed out water as fast as you can. You've tried to patch leaks. You've thrown all the cargo you can out of your life, but your boat is full and a wave away from being swallowed up.

In a certain sense, by nature we are all in a storm. We may be insensitive to it—we may be blind to the waves, deaf to the wind, and unaware of our danger—but Satan is about to swallow us up. We have no safe ground under our feet, and there is just a wave between us and death. Many are asleep, as

Jonah was, seemingly oblivious to the fact that they are about to sink. If only we would see what the disciples saw and begin to cry as they did!

The disciples didn't try to awaken Jesus immediately. They must have assumed that He would wake up at some point. There is no record of them coming to Him until the ship was full. No matter what they did, however, nothing changed for the better until these disciples went to the Lord and took Him by the shoulder like men who were desperate. By this time, they meant business. They awakened Him and said, "Master, carest thou not that we perish?" (Mark 4:38).

The disciples' question here shows their confusion. They are perplexed about how Christ could be so insensitive. But how could Christ be oblivious and uncaring? Here are some important thoughts Jesus' disciples should have remembered, and present disciples who are enduring any kind of "storm" will find them helpful as well:

- Christ has brought us into this trouble. After all, He commanded us to enter the boat. Since He has been directly instrumental in ordering this circumstance, He must be well aware of our distress.

- Christ's words imply a safe arrival on the other side of the lake: "Let us pass over *unto the other side*" (Mark 4:35, emphasis added). He knew that they would reach the other side. (Present-day disciples should also be comforted by this truth. If you are a child of God, there is another side to your sickness, your family problem, your convicted conscience, or your heartache. There is another

side even to death, which Christ Himself brought
to light in His resurrection. Jesus will ensure your
safe arrival on the other side.)

- Even Jesus' sleeping should be a lesson to us. Quite
possibly, Jesus slept to teach us that sleep is possible even in the fiercest storm. As David said in
Psalm 3: "I laid me down and slept; I awaked; for
the LORD sustained me" (v. 5).

Powerful Lessons

The Lord was teaching His disciples a lesson even in His
sleep, but He would teach them a much greater lesson by
waking *from* sleep. This waking radically transformed the
disciples' situation. "He arose, and rebuked the wind, and
said unto the sea, Peace, be still" (Mark 4:39). There are four
brief lessons here.

First, we see the lesson of *Christ's power.* Asleep one
moment and awake the next, Christ spoke with authority to
the wind and waves. Literally, Jesus said, "Be mute! Be muzzled!" With His words He muzzled the gaping sea. What
power! What authority! Christ's divinity enabled Him to
speak with this kind of authority.

Second is the lesson of *Christ's purpose.* "There was a
great calm" (Mark 4:39). Christ's purpose was to bring the
disciples into a great calm. He rebuked the storm not just
because He is divine and powerful, but also to reveal His
purpose. He had come from heaven to this tumultuous
world to pay for and take away the cause of all the trouble—
namely, sin. Think of the storm into which Christ would

soon willingly go—the raging sea of God's wrath on Calvary. Moreover, after His death and burial, He would arise from the "sleep" of death. Mark says, "He arose" (4:39), just as He *rose* again from the grave (1 Cor. 15:4).

Dear friend, are you in a storm now? Is Satan accusing you? Is the world buffeting you? Is your conscience a tempest? There is no calm like the calm Christ brings when He speaks peace to your storm-tossed soul. This Admiral will bring you safely into the harbor. A common saying of the past sums it up well: He has not promised a calm journey, but He will give a safe arrival. He has invested everything in you and shed His blood for you. He will not leave you in the storm, but will bring you safely to land. He cares for you. You will not perish.

Third, we learn about the lesson of the *Christian's posture*. Christ was teaching the disciples how to handle difficult circumstances. Their approach should have been one of faith, not fear: "Why are ye so fearful? how is it that ye have no faith?" (Mark 4:40). Remember this if you are struggling with storms in your life: walk by faith, not by sight. Christ can silence the storms as no one else can. He can bring calm to your troubled heart. He can bring courage to those who are faint. He can silence the accusing conscience. He can give you this posture by His grace and Holy Spirit.

Finally, we can learn here about the lesson of *the Christian's praise*. The Lord calls us to a posture of awe and reverence for Him. Notice how the disciples praise Him by saying, "What manner of man is this, that even the wind and the sea obey him?" (Mark 4:41). The Lord calls us to awe and reverence Him in the same way. This was no normal man;

this was the God-man. Imagine if the Lord had never brought His disciples into the storm. They wouldn't have been able to praise Him to the same degree. In a sense, heaven will be one long, unending, "What manner of man—what manner of God-man—is this?"

Is Christ on board the ship of your life? If not, the disciples' question to Christ could be put to you: Don't you care that you are perishing? Do you have an Admiral to lead you? You are a mere human being! The wind and the waves will not listen to you, especially not the waves of God's just judgment over your sin. Cry out to this infinitely capable Admiral who has proven Himself under the billows of wrath. Say with the poet:

> Jesus, Savior, pilot me,
> Over life's tempestuous sea;
> Unknown waves before me roll,
> Hiding rock and treacherous shoal.
> Chart and compass come from Thee;
> Jesus, Savior, pilot me.[5]

Only He can silence the final storm of God's wrath that is about to break out over sinners. Yet, through the power of His voice, you too can reach the other side, where all God's true disciples will sing out forever: "What manner of man is this!"

Questions

1. For further study: you can read about this miracle in Matthew 8:23–27 and Luke 8:22–25 also.

2. Unlike with Jonah, a storm met the disciples in the way of obedience. How can we know whether the storms God sends us in life are to chastise us or to test us?

3. Read Psalm 107:23–30. Find five parallels between these verses and Mark 4:35–41. What does this comparison prove to us about the person of Christ?

4. Look up Acts 12:5. What lessons had Peter learned by this time that enabled him to be like his Master in the storm? What does it look like for you to sleep through some of the storms in your life? Give an example if you can.

5. What practical significance do you find in the little word "full" in Mark 4:37? Why do we often wait until the problems are "up to the brim" in our lives to ask for God's help? Why might God often wait until our problems are so many that we can't handle them to help us?

6. How can you help a child of God who is questioning the Lord's care and concern, as the disciples did in Mark 4:38?

7. What do you think about the way the disciples adored Christ in Mark 4:41? Which of the following words summarizes your thoughts: enviable,

desirable, practical, out of reach, convicting? Are there other words that more accurately reflect your reaction?

8. Has God sent storms in your life? If so, can you reflect on God's role in the storm?

9

The Healing of the Gadarene Demoniac

Mark 5:1–20

[Jesus] saith unto him, Go home to thy friends, and tell them how great things the Lord hath done for thee, and hath had compassion on thee. And he departed, and began to publish in Decapolis how great things Jesus had done for him: and all men did marvel.

—MARK 5:19–20

Our society is obsessed with darkness, death, and devils, especially at certain times of the year such as Halloween. Around Halloween, you can hardly go into stores or down the street without seeing a display of ghosts, goblins, and gravestones. Some might think of it as innocent fun, but one of my students from Africa, speaking of witchcraft, asked, "Why would Americans joke about something that kills thousands of people in my country and keeps hundreds of thousands in bondage and darkness?"

Increasingly, books and films thrust upon our culture focus on vampires, witches, terror, and death. Is this not paving a return to the darkness of paganism, where devils and darkness are welcome and the teachings of Christianity are no longer tolerated, but resisted? Will this usher in the return of the bondage that reigned for many centuries before the light of the gospel shone widely throughout western Europe and America? It certainly seems like it.

What will loosen the hold of darkness as it comes creeping up on our own country? Who can save us from the devil's influence, which so many seem to be courting? Is there a force stronger than the devil? Christ's miracle in Gadara proves that there is One who is not only stronger than the devil, but who acts in compassion and mercy to save from the devil's grip.

A Satanic Reaction

The Lord Jesus and His twelve disciples had just crossed the Sea of Galilee. During that crossing, Christ had done a great miracle, calming the raging of the sea. The disciples had been left awestruck: "What manner of man is this, that even the wind and the sea obey him?" (Mark 4:41). On the other side of the sea, Christ met not the power of a force of creation, but the prince of the power of the air (Eph. 2:2).

Mark 5 tells us that Jesus and His disciples landed in the region of the Gadarenes, the area around the city of Gadara. This was also known as the Decapolis region on the east side of the Jordan and the Sea of Galilee. The people here were not Jews, but Gentiles. The region was known for its hog farming. This was something anathema to the Jews, for, according to the stipulations of Mosaic law, pigs were unclean animals. This area was also occupied by the Romans, who would march through the region regularly, pillaging homes and cities and keeping the people in subservient fear.

The people were also afraid of one of their own citizens—a demon-possessed man, if you could even call him a man. It seems he had enjoyed normal relationships with others at one time, for after Christ healed him, he would go home to his friends (Mark 5:19). But this man had become so controlled by demons that he was unrecognizable to his friends and family. Mark 5:9 tells us that he was possessed by a legion of demons. A legion is a fearsome unit—a Roman legion, for example, may have been composed of thousands of foot soldiers and a couple hundred cavalry. Clearly this man was completely uncontrollable. In fact, when people tried to restrain him with chains, he would snap the chains and continue his raging (Mark 5:4). What a sad picture Mark paints of him: "Always, night and day, he was in the mountains, and in the tombs, crying, and cutting himself with stones" (5:5). Mark also writes that he "had his dwelling among the tombs" (5:3). Luke tells us that he went around without clothes, striking fear into the heart of any traveler who came within hearing distance.

The devil always works to destroy—and what a picture this man was of the devil's work. He loves nothing better than to steal, kill, and destroy (John 10:10). So this poor man, a captive of the prince of the power of the air (Heb. 2:14), brought fear to this whole area.

Thankfully, in this account another prince—the Prince of Life—arrived on the shores of this area. You might say that He was coming into enemy territory. When Jesus landed on the shore, it seems this man saw Him coming from a distance and began to run wildly at full speed down the hill toward Him, crying out, "What have I to do with thee, Jesus, thou Son of the most high God?" (Mark 5:7).

What a strange mixture of *aggression* and *reverence* in this man. We can understand the hostility, for what greater opposites could there be than light and darkness—Christ and Satan? But, at the same time, the man fell at the feet of Christ, the verse tells us, in a prostrate position, doing obeisance to Him. If this seems surprising, remember that James tells us that the devils believe and tremble (2:19). They do what many human beings never think to do—tremble before the majesty of Christ. Notice also that the demons acknowledged Christ for who He is—the Son of God. Moreover, they spoke about hell as a real place of torment (see Mark 5:7). This satanic reaction to Christ teaches us that one day, every knee will bow (Phil. 2:10–11). How necessary it is to learn to bow now in the day of grace when we have opportunity to be reconciled to Him!

The Man's Restoration

We have to say that the afflicted man was hardly acting as a living human being at this point. For all intents and purposes, his life was a living hell. He lived on the brink of the abyss. What mercy when Christ delivered him from such a desperate state!

Notice, first, *how the restoration of this man proved Christ's royal power*. He did not need to use ceremonies or rituals in exorcising these demons. He did not need battering rams and cannons to defeat this legion of devils. As the King of kings and Lord of lords, He is more than thousands of foot soldiers and hundreds of cavalry. He simply spoke one command: "Come out of the man, thou unclean spirit" (Mark 5:8).

These demons responded to Christ's command by begging not to be sent directly into hell, but instead to enter into the pigs (Mark 5:12). Some may wonder whether this meant that Christ's words did not have immediate effect. But what Christ did actually proved and displayed His power all the more, for if these demons were capable of driving a herd of two thousand pigs down a cliff into the sea, they must have been absolutely ferocious inside this man. What power Christ had to dismiss a legion this large!

Notice, second, that *the restoration of this man shows Christ's priestly compassion.* Thousands of pigs can't match the worth of one soul! How true Jesus' words: "What shall it profit a man, if he shall gain the whole world, and lose his own soul?" (Mark 8:36). The Lord's allowing the demons to go into these pigs shows how precious a soul is to Him. It is above the value of anything and everything.

Christ Himself attributed this miracle to His compassion. He tells the man in verse 19, after all is said and done, "Go home to thy friends, and tell them how great things the Lord hath done for thee, *and hath had compassion on thee*" (emphasis added). It was not only power that set this man free; it was also compassion, mercy, divine love. The Lord met devilish force with divine force, but He also met this miserable man with mercy. He pitied him. Truly Christ is our High Priest, "who can have compassion…on them that are out of the way" (Heb. 5:2).

The Citizens' Rejection

One might expect that the citizens of the area, who witnessed what Christ did for this man, would fall at Christ's feet in awe and gratitude. Finally, an uncontrollable legion of devils had been expelled! This man, their old friend and neighbor, had been restored to them. With their own eyes, they saw that he was "sitting, and clothed, and in his right mind" (Mark 5:15). We might expect that they would have implored the Lord Jesus to have compassion on them as well.

We read that the people were "afraid" after witnessing this miracle (Mark 5:15). They realized something great had happened. They were in awe, but their awe did not bring them to the feet of Christ. Instead, "they began to pray him to depart out of their coasts" (Mark 5:17). What a contrast to the restored man, who "prayed him that he might be with him" (Mark 5:18). What opposite reactions to this display of Christ's power and mercy!

What is your response to Christ? The Scriptures reveal this power and mercy. Have you come to need this Christ and His strong compassion? His compassion is strong enough for the worst and most wretched of sinners. He can keep you from going down to this pit, as we read in Job 33:24: "Then he is gracious unto him, and saith, Deliver him from going down to the pit: I have found a ransom."

This compassionate High Priest is Himself the ransom. As the Prince of Life, He descended into hell on the cross in order to do battle with the devil and make a show of him openly (see Col. 2:15). And so we sing with great confidence, from the time of the Reformation till today, of Christ's great victory:

> And tho' this world, with devils filled,
> Should threaten to undo us,
> We will not fear, for God hath willed
> His truth to triumph thro' us.
> The prince of darkness grim,

We tremble not for him;
His rage we can endure,
For lo, his doom is sure,
One little word shall fell him.[6]

Questions

1. For further study: you can read about this miracle in Matthew 8:28–34 and Luke 8:26–39 also.

2. Do you find people around you more and more obsessed with the powers of darkness? What posture should we have toward the devil and the occult? What does this passage in Mark 5 help us see about the reality of the devil, hell, and Christ?

3. What can we learn from how these demons approached Christ?

4. What practical and spiritual lessons can we learn from Christ's allowing the demons to go into the pigs?

5. Christ's words could do more than the chains that the people used to try to bind this man. What does this tell us about the power of Christ's word today?

6. The citizens wanted Jesus at a safe distance, not interfering with their daily lives. What are some of the more subtle ways we can display this attitude in our churches and communities or personal lives?

7. How is it comforting to know that Christ is both a powerful Prince and a compassionate High Priest?

10

The Woman with the Issue of Blood

Mark 5:25–34

[Jesus] said unto her, Daughter, thy faith hath made thee whole; go in peace, and be whole of thy plague.
—MARK 5:34

The miraculous healing of the woman with the issue of blood took place at the same time as the raising of Jairus's daughter, which we will look at in the next chapter. Three of the Gospels place the two miracles together. We don't know if Jairus and the woman ever got together to reflect on their miracles, but the Lord often brings people together and then works so that they can take encouragement from one another about what He is doing in their lives. The woman could have been encouraged that Jesus was going with Jairus; Jairus could have taken encouragement from Jesus' stopping on the way to give someone else a complete healing.

It is interesting that the woman had been suffering from her illness for twelve years—the age of Jairus's daughter. The young girl was at the point of death, and the woman was not far behind. But beyond these similarities, there were differences between the circumstances of Jairus and the woman. Jairus was chief of the synagogue, a public figure in his town.

He walked up to Jesus and gave an eloquent request: "My little daughter lieth at the point of death: I pray thee, come and lay thy hands on her, that she may be healed; and she shall live" (Mark 5:23). The woman, on the other hand, remains nameless in Scripture. Considered unclean, she came from behind to reach out and touch the hem of Christ's garment, then tried to steal away quietly. Though the woman and Jairus were so different and came so differently, Christ's grace acted powerfully for both of them as a testimony to what His grace can do for all kinds of people.

The Trouble

We aren't told exactly what the woman's disease was. Whatever it was caused incessant bleeding—day in and day out. The effects of this constant loss of blood must have been debilitating. Genesis 9:4 tells us that life is in the blood; this woman felt as if life was constantly ebbing from her. Her pale complexion and physical weakness must have been obvious to anyone who could get a good look at her.

According to Leviticus 15:25–27, this woman, because of her illness, would have been shunned as well as barred from the temple. If anyone touched what she had touched, he or she would be unclean. How she must have wept to read Scripture's verdict: "She shall be unclean." Certainly viewed from this angle, her sickness was what our passage calls a "plague" (Mark 5:29; literally, "stroke," "scourge," or "whip").

Humanly speaking, the woman had tried everything in her search for a cure. She had consulted many doctors. She must have originally been a woman of some wealth, but she had spent all she had upon physicians. Mark says she "had suffered many things of many physicians" (5:26). The people who were to relieve suffering actually intensified it for her. Not only her blood but also her resources were being drained, and she was no better, "but rather grew worse" (5:26).

The Levitical requirements that God laid upon the people of Israel were meant to teach them the seriousness of sin. Does not sin defile us and render us unclean and vile? It saps our strength and vitality, our joy and peace, and, above all, separates us from each other and from God (see Isa. 59:2). Whatever earthly doctors we consult for help and healing, our sinful disease is none the better.

News of a greater Physician reached this woman's ears, however (Mark 5:27). Perhaps the report that Christ had touched the unclean leper and healed him awakened hope in her otherwise despairing heart. With her desperate need driving her on the one hand, and the report of Christ's ability drawing her on the other, she went to Christ. Behind this woman's coming, however, was the Father drawing her to the feet of His Son (John 6:44). She came with hope, however faint, of finding a way of escape from twelve years of misery.

The Touch

The woman made her way through the crowd to the Lord's side. She undoubtedly came with both stealth and determination. According to the text in the original language, she kept saying to herself, "If I may touch but his clothes" (Mark 5:28). As she moved through the crowds inch by inch, she came to the point where she could see Christ's garment. We know from John 19 that Christ's outer coat was seamless, of one piece.

This woman clearly had high regard for Christ. She recognized that just touching the hem of this glorious person could bring healing. For twelve long years, she hadn't been allowed to touch anyone or anyone's clothing without making that person unclean, but how inexorably she felt drawn to touch this Savior!

The word "touched" in the original refers to a determined hold, not just a passing brush. This woman's hold on Christ brought about what we read in Mark 5:29: "Straightway the fountain of her blood was dried up; and she felt in her body that she was healed of that plague." In other words, the woman's disease disappeared in a moment—not just the symptoms, but all the way back to the very root. The cause of her seclusion, her uncleanness, her shame was gone.

How could Jesus do this? He could do it because He had come to take care of the root problem—namely, sin. Power issued forth from Him to deal with the uncleanness issuing from her. Zechariah 13:1 had prophesied, "In that day there shall be a fountain opened to the house of David and to the inhabitants of Jerusalem for sin and for uncleanness." Like what we read in Ezekiel 16:6, Jesus' power reached her as she was there, wallowing in her own blood, and said to her, "Live."

And live she did. Gone were the days when life was ebbing away from her—all because she had touched the hem of the Savior's garment. This miracle proclaims to us the mediatorial power of Christ to deal effectively with the plague of our sin through His death and resurrection. Shouldn't we stir ourselves up to take hold of God's Son by faith for salvation? Isaiah 64:7 says: "And there is none that calleth upon thy name, that stirreth up himself to take hold of thee: for thou hast hid thy face from us, and hast consumed us, because of our iniquities." Many simply crowd around Christ without taking hold of Him by faith; they do not understand their need or estimate His ability to save to the uttermost. May that never be said of us!

Some have compared the promises of the gospel to the hem of Christ's garment, which unclean sinners may take hold of. When they do, God in Christ conveys what no other physician can: spiritual healing, restoration, and power for new life. Let us take a lesson from the faith of this woman. She didn't ask anything of Jesus or claim anything. Yet she believed that simply touching His clothes was enough to heal her.

The Teacher

It is interesting to notice that Christ was not satisfied with impersonally healing this woman. He wanted contact with her. The Savior healed her, but then He also proceeded to teach her. Mark 5:30 reads: "And Jesus, immediately knowing in himself that virtue had gone out of him, turned him about in the press, and said, Who touched my clothes?"

This question strikes us as strange, given the large crowd pressing in on Christ. Peter asked him why He would ask. In fact, in Luke we read that all denied it (8:45). But the same Christ who knew Nathanael under the fig tree and Zacchaeus in the sycamore tree also knew exactly who this woman was. He certainly recognized that someone had touched Him. Christ recognizes the touch of faith, and among the hundreds of people pressing Him, Jesus could sense the one believing touch among them all. This woman came secretly to Jesus, and He had allowed it; but she would not leave secretly. Christ would not let her go quietly back to her home, only to doubt and fear whether what she had done was wrong. He would bless her further. Thus His searching question: "Who touched my clothes?" (Mark 5:30).

Christ's question and His subsequent words to her were the means for Him to seal His work in her, the kind of thing Paul refers to in Ephesians 1:13 when he writes to the believers there about their salvation. He reminds them that after they believed, they were "sealed with that holy Spirit of promise." In this specific case, Christ did three things that parallel what He does in the life of every person He is saving.

First, He saw her. "He looked round about to see her that had done this thing" (Mark 5:32). This is like the bridegroom calling to see His bride, as we read in Song of Solomon 2:14: "O my dove, that art in the clefts of the rock, in the secret places of the stairs, let me see thy countenance, let me hear thy voice; for sweet is thy voice, and thy countenance is comely." He calls secret believers out into the open where He can teach them and bestow more blessings on them.

Second, He brought her to confess Him. Paul says: "For with the heart man believeth unto righteousness; and with the mouth confession is made unto salvation" (Rom. 10:10). Christ brought the woman to confess, even with fear and trembling. So it is every time the Lord assures and seals His power in the lives of His people.

Finally, He instructed her. Christ's words in Mark 5:34 contain much instruction for this woman and for all true believers: "Daughter, thy faith hath made thee whole; go in peace, and be whole of thy plague." Every phrase is almost like a chapter heading for the Christian's identity, life, and future. In the Old Testament, this woman would have needed to be declared clean by the priest (Lev. 15:29–30). Here, Christ is much greater than any other priest. He both healed her and declared her clean. No wonder the Bible says in Hebrews 4:15: "We have not an high priest which cannot be touched with the feeling of our infirmities." Like this woman, let us go boldly to Him in the gospel that we may obtain mercy and find grace to help in time of need.

Questions

1. For further study: you can read about this miracle in Matthew 9:20–22 and Luke 8:43–48 also.

2. Are there any similarities between this woman's trouble and trouble you may find yourself in? What part of her story can you most relate to?

3. Sometimes people are afraid of "stealing" a blessing that might not be theirs. What insight does this passage give about that—not only in the beginning but also at the end?

4. In Isaiah 64:7, the prophet laments that so few stir themselves up to take hold of the Lord. Do you know what it means to take hold of the Lord? How can you know that you have done so?

5. Elaborate on everything the Savior teaches the woman in verse 34. Can you see any parallels with what the Lord may have done for you?

6. Discuss whether there is such a thing as a secret disciple, and, if so, what needs to happen to that person. In addition to this miracle, consult John 19:38–39.

11

The Raising of Jairus's Daughter

Luke 8:41–42, 49–56

[Jesus]…called, saying, Maid, arise. And her spirit came again, and she arose straightway.
—LUKE 8:54–55

In the last chapter, we noted that the woman with the issue of blood and Jairus experienced the Lord's miraculous ability around the same time. In fact, the two would be remembered in the Gospels together, side by side. Although it must have been hard for Jairus to have to wait while Jesus healed the woman, he would benefit from the interruption in the long run. He would be taught patience, and he would therein receive a greater answer to prayer than he initially had even hoped. Most importantly, he would learn more about the Lord Jesus Christ.

The Trouble

Jairus held an important position in Israel. The Bible calls him a ruler of the synagogue. This would have been quite an honor, even in a small town like Galilee. In essence, he was something of a head elder, executing the policies of the synagogue. He also controlled who would speak in his synagogue.

We don't know what Jairus thought of Jesus before the time of this narrative. If he was like the other rulers of the synagogue, he may have had his doubts. He may have wanted to avoid the controversy that would undoubtedly accompany Jesus should He come to his synagogue.

If these things were true, everything changed one day when his only daughter, who was twelve years old, became sick. Apparently none of the local doctors were able to help. No matter what Jairus tried, things went from bad to worse. His daughter soon reached the point of death. So when Jairus heard that Jesus was coming to his area, he hurried out to meet Him and "fell down at Jesus' feet" (Luke 8:41).

Picture Jairus prostrating himself before Christ. Pouring out his need before the Lord, he pleaded with Christ to come to his house and lay His hands on his daughter (Mark 5:23) so that she might be healed. Jairus went so far as to specify how Christ should perform this healing. And yet, Christ did not reprove him, but agreed to go along with him (Luke 8:42). How willing Christ is to help those who have no other helper!

The Test

The delay that Jairus had to endure as Jesus stopped to heal the woman with the issue of blood must have been a nail-biting experience for him. After all, every minute counted. Perhaps his anxiety turned to panic when, off in the distance, he saw someone come running. His worst fear was confirmed by this messenger: it was too late. His precious, only daughter was dead. He had failed in his attempt to save her. What grief must have rushed over Jairus in that moment!

What a temptation this must have been for Jairus to despair! Perhaps the messenger's words only rubbed it in: "Trouble not the Master" (Luke 8:49). There are times in life when well-meaning people give us advice, but their advice is not mixed with faith. And the Bible teaches us that whatever is not of faith is sin (Rom. 14:23). Granted, we have no right to expect that God will perform a miracle in answer to our requests. But still, the question remains: Does unbelief triumph over faith in our hearts when seemingly impossible circumstances invade our lives? Or do we listen to the voice of Christ, who said to Jairus: "Fear not: believe only" (Luke 8:50)? The Lord was propping up Jairus's sinking faith, for He knew the thoughts of this father's heart. With the power of His word, He resurrected Jairus's faith before He resurrected Jairus's daughter.

The Triumphant One

Hearing the news of the girl's death, Christ directed His steps toward the home of Jairus. The place certainly had the look and sound of death about it. The presence of professional mourners seemed to confirm the stark reality. The laughter and scorn they directed toward Christ reveal how pathetic they were (Luke 8:53). At any rate, Christ sent them away. He allowed only three disciples and Jairus and his wife to be in the girl's room.

For Christ, death is no more powerful than sleep. He explained it that way Himself (Luke 8:52). Christ simply needs to stir the dead, and death is shaken off like sleep. That is exactly what happened to Jairus's daughter. Jesus took her by the hand and said: "Maid, arise" (Luke 8:54). Mark records it like this: "Talitha cumi; which is, being interpreted, Damsel, I say unto thee, arise" (Mark 5:41). Death could not hold her in its grasp when the triumphant One awoke her. What a confirmation of life when Christ told her parents to give her something to eat (Luke 8:55)!

Christ's power triumphed over death, not just because He is the Son of God but as a foreshadowing of what He would do in His death on the cross. There He would "destroy him that had the power of death, that is, the devil; and deliver them who through fear of death were all their lifetime subject to bondage" (Heb. 2:14–15).

This raised little twelve-year-old girl was a wondrous sign to behold. Like a living parable of Christ's coming victory, she, as it were, arose from sleep by the touch and hand of Jesus. Paul tells us that for believers who die, it is as if they fall asleep in Jesus (1 Thess. 4:14). At the resurrection, their bodies will awaken much like this young girl's did. Daniel 12:2 pictures it like this: "Many of them that sleep in the dust of the earth shall awake." What a day that will be!

Death is the last enemy, but it is not the final victor. One day, returning on the clouds, Christ, by His almighty word, will open the graves of all His sleeping children, and through resurrection power He will raise them to life forevermore.

Questions

1. For further study: you can read about this miracle in Matthew 9:18–26 and Mark 5:22–24 also.

2. How do you think that Jairus benefited from the interruption of the woman with the issue of blood? Can you give any examples of how God's delays in your life may have turned out for your good, even though at the time it looked disastrous? What does this tell us about God's timing and ours?

3. The man from Jairus's house told Jairus not to trouble Christ. Do you ever tell yourself that? Can you see from this miracle what actually troubles Christ, and what does not?

4. Why do you think Christ refused to do the miracle in front of the mocking crowd? What does this tell us our attitude should be if we wish to see Christ at work?

5. In a way, the miracle that Christ did in Jairus's heart was as important as what He did to Jairus's daughter. How might we experience what Jairus experienced, even if God does not drive sickness and death away from us?

6. Christ did not limit His miracles to adults; the text mentions explicitly that Jairus's daughter was only twelve years old. Imagine yourself talking to a group of twelve-year-olds. What could you tell them about what Christ says to them through this story?

12

The Feeding of the Five Thousand

Mark 6:31–44

When [Jesus] had taken the five loaves and the two fishes, he looked up to heaven, and blessed, and brake the loaves, and gave them to his disciples to set before them; and the two fishes divided he among them all. And they did all eat, and were filled.

—MARK 6:41–42

For parents in many parts of our world today, filling the empty stomachs of their families is a struggle. We who live in highly privileged areas of the West often fail to recognize what a pressing need physical hunger is. On a deeper level, countless people in our world have hungry hearts, minds, and souls, lacking what is truly necessary and truly satisfying in life on an emotional and spiritual level. How much emptiness sin has brought into this world! At some level, hunger stares all of us in the face. None of us has what it takes to provide for our own bodies and souls, much less for the needs of others. We are so dependent on God, the source of all good things! And He is so able and willing to provide for our every need, as we see in the miracle of the feeding of the five thousand.

Neglected Sheep

This is the only miracle recorded in all four gospels. It took place around the time of the Passover (John 6:4). After a busy season of ministry in and around Capernaum, Christ and His disciples had boarded a boat in order to retreat for a while. They traveled about four or five miles, directly across the lake, to the area of Bethsaida (Luke 9:10). After people saw the Lord Jesus and His disciples coming off the boat, news quickly spread, and they came from all directions to gather around the Savior (Mark 6:33). Moved with compassion, Christ taught the people. He perceived that they were like sheep without a shepherd who needed spiritual direction and guidance (Matt. 9:36). Mark tells us, "He began to teach them many things" (6:34). Luke mentions that He "spake unto them of the kingdom of God," and He accompanied His words with signs, healing those in need (9:11). Clearly, the Lord would give Himself no rest until He had fed these neglected sheep with spiritual food.

Short-Sighted Disciples

When we put the various gospel accounts alongside each other, especially Mark and John, we notice that Christ prepared His disciples for this miracle in two steps. First, as the Lord Jesus saw the large crowd that was gathering, He asked Philip a telling question: "Whence shall we buy bread, that these may eat?" (John 6:5). John tells us that Jesus asked this in order to prove Philip, "for he himself knew what he would do" (6:6). In other words, Jesus was preparing the way for the miracle He would do. It was Philip who had once confessed: "We have found the Messias, which is, being interpreted, the

Christ" (John 1:41). Sadly, at this moment Philip focused on the practicalities of the situation rather than on the almighty power of the Messiah who was with him. He answered the Lord: "Two hundred pennyworth [or denarii, the daily wage for a day laborer] of bread is not sufficient for them, that every one of them may take a little" (John 6:7). It would take a lot of money, Philip was saying, to feed a crowd this large. But as the hours wore on, it must have become obvious to the disciples that, in addition to the spiritual food Christ was providing, these people would need physical food. They urged the Lord to "send them away, that they may go into the country round about, and into the villages, and buy themselves bread" (Mark 6:36). Perhaps the disciples were weary of the crowd and were eager for it to disperse. Perhaps they didn't want to deal with the situation that might develop if the multitude was allowed to grow too hungry. At any rate, they suggested that the crowd be sent away.

Instead of sending the people off to find their own food, Jesus now gave His disciples an explicit direction: "Give ye them to eat" (Mark 6:37). How could Jesus ask them to provide food for such a large crowd? If only they had recognized His prompting to look to Him to supply this need! Andrew did report that there was a boy in the crowd who had five barley loaves and two small fish, but he could not see what good such a small amount of food would do: "What are they among so many?" (John 6:9). It is clear that the faith of the disciples was not in exercise as it should have been. If only their eyes had been focused on Christ rather than on the circumstances, they might have eagerly anticipated His miraculous help.

Do we recognize our own thoughts in the words of Philip and Andrew? Often, like the disciples, we would rather that God "send away" our problems than that He would glorify His greatness through them. Our limited human understanding so often fails to see the divine possibilities that present themselves in our impossibilities! How small our thoughts are, and how quickly we reach the end of our reasoning! If only we looked more to God, whose thoughts are much higher than ours (Isa. 55:8–9).

How the disciples might have benefited from remembering the Lord's mighty deeds in the past! If they had remembered how Joseph had fed all of Egypt from His storehouses of grain (Gen. 41:55), they might have looked to this greater Joseph for provision. If they had remembered God's provision of manna in the wilderness (Ex. 16:14–15), they might have expected an abundant supply of food here as well. If they had remembered God's promise that He could open the windows of heaven and give a blessing too great to contain (Mal. 3:10), they might have prayed for God to rend the heavens. These men had been eyewitnesses of Christ's miracle at the wedding in Cana, when He had provided a miraculous supply of wine for the guests. If only they would have looked in expectant faith to Him, of whom we read: "The eyes of all wait upon thee; and thou givest them their meat in due season. Thou openest thine hand, and satisfieth the desire of every living thing" (Ps. 145:15–16).

A Glorious Shepherd

Christ would magnify His glory by using a humble meal to provide for this large crowd—a meal furnished by the heavenly King, but not according to the standards of earthly kings. Barley loaves were hard, flat cakes and were considered the food of the poor. The fish, which would most likely have been dried or roasted, would help make the bread more tasty and nutritious. And yet this miracle would be evidence that Christ chooses "the base things of the world, and things which are despised" to exalt His glory (1 Cor. 1:28).

Christ commanded the disciples to have the crowd sit down. He would do His work in an orderly fashion, and so He instructed that the people sit down "by companies" (Mark 6:39). The people sat down "in ranks, by hundreds, and by fifties" (Mark 6:40). This way the disciples could move in aisles through the groups of people to distribute the food. In the original, the word "ranks" suggests the picture of a garden bed. The orderly God of creation, who had fashioned the flowers, herbs, and grasses, would now tend His spiritual garden for the glory of His Father.

Christ did not proceed without looking "up to heaven" (Mark 6:41), thus thanking His Father (John 6:11) and blessing the food (Mark 6:41). What a reminder of Paul's teaching: "Whether therefore ye eat, or drink...do all to the glory of God" (1 Cor. 10:31). Then, quietly and gently, as He broke the bread, the miracle happened as the bread multiplied. The Savior kept distributing food to the disciples, who in turn passed it out to the hungry multitude.

A Satisfied People

Centuries before, manna from heaven had continually sustained millions of hungry Israelites in the desert. Now, through His incarnate Son, God had again spread a table in the wilderness and was filling hungry hearts. All five thousand men, plus women and children, were plentifully fed from a poor boy's lunch.

What an instructive event this was for the disciples! After initially wanting to send the people away, they were now learning to serve the people out of Christ's fullness. Each time they ran out of supplies, they had only to run back to Christ to receive fresh supplies to put into the hands of these needy people. Can't you imagine them watching Christ dividing up this poor boy's lunch and watching it grow? Natural processes that normally took a season to complete—sowing seed, growing grain, harvesting, threshing, and baking bread—were compressed into a second under the mighty hands of the Word made flesh. What normally takes place over a span of months in the hidden recesses of the Sea of Galilee—fish hatching, maturing, and then being caught by toiling fishermen—all took place instantaneously in the hand of the Creator, who had formed the sea and dry land and filled them with life.

Near the seaside that day, the people's hunger was satisfied. We read that "they...were filled" (Mark 6:42). Mark also tells us that the leftovers from the meal were enough to fill twelve baskets full (6:43). Surely, when God fills the hungry with good things, He satisfies them. His supplies are overflowing!

What thoughts would have been on your mind that evening if you had been in the crowd that was gathered, as you looked out toward the setting sun over the shimmery Sea of Galilee? The next day, Christ would teach the people with these words: "I am the bread of life: he that cometh to me shall never hunger; and he that believeth on me shall never thirst" (John 6:35). Those words should have had rich meaning for anyone who had been witness to this miracle. Do we receive the food God daily supplies us with as a miracle? When we sit "rank and file" in our various houses of worship, do we receive the spiritual food God has appointed for us through His ministers with thanksgiving and awe (see 1 Peter 5:2)?

On the cross Christ did so much more than break a boy's poor lunch; He Himself was broken in order that He might feed souls empty of righteousness and life with Himself. There He was so much more than the Creator; He was the Redeemer. On Calvary, He didn't simply create food, but He re-created people whom He has formed for His praise. By His grace and Holy Spirit, He empties them of their pride and self-righteousness and fills them with Himself. With Him as their shepherd, they have no wants (Ps. 23:1). They learn more and more what it is to be satisfied with Him. Have you tasted and come to know this all-sufficient Mediator?

Questions

1. For further study: you can read about this miracle in Matthew 14:13–21; Luke 9:10–17; and John 6:11–13 also.

2. What are the qualities of a good shepherd (see John 10:10–15), and why didn't the scribes and Pharisees fit this description? Compare this with Ezekiel 34:12. How do we come under the care of the Good Shepherd?

3. How did Jesus test the faith of Philip? Why did He do that? What is the importance of our having faith while we look for Christ's gifts?

4. What does this passage tell us about the care of Christ for our bodies and souls? Is there a promise for us in this?

5. Read Mark 6:41. How can this attitude of Jesus toward God's gifts and blessings help us to glorify God? Will that change our attitude toward the things we possess? How?

6. Have you ever felt that worries about practical things of daily life supersede your spiritual life? How can this passage help you with this?

7. What does this passage tell us about the way the Lord provides (Mark 6:43)? How can we have a daily dependency on the gifts of God, and how can this strengthen our faith?

13

Walking on the Water

Matthew 14:22–33

> *But the ship was now in the midst of the sea, tossed with waves: for the wind was contrary. And in the fourth watch of the night Jesus went unto them, walking on the sea.*
> —MATTHEW 14:24–25

One way for God's people to understand their difficult experiences is to see them as times between deliverances. Paul writes to the Corinthians that God "delivered us from so great a death, and doth deliver: in whom we trust that he will yet deliver us" (2 Cor. 1:10). In other words, God delivers His people again and again. They have no reason to doubt their ultimate safety. And yet, between those deliverances, God tests and stretches the faith of His people through trials in order that they would learn to love Him more, follow Him more closely, rely on His word more exclusively, and glorify their Savior more heartily and deeply. The miracle we are about to consider illustrates this truth for us.

Purposeful Constraint

This passage immediately follows the account of the miraculous feeding of the five thousand. What a spectacular event that had been! Enthralled with that display of Christ's power, the crowds were clamoring to make Him a national king (John 6:15). But a crown without a cross was not the purpose for which Christ had come.

In Matthew 14:22 we read that Jesus "constrained" His disciples to get into a ship without Him. He would join them later after spending time alone with His Father (Matt. 14:23; John 6:15). This may not have been what the disciples were expecting, and so they may have been disappointed and confused by Christ's wishes. But Christ had His plans and purposes for sending them off in their boat. He knew all about the storm they would encounter there.

Soon, the calm weather changed, and it wasn't long before the disciples knew that they were in deep trouble. From the time references in the text we learn that, in the space of the next six hours, they were able to cover a distance of only about three miles. Their night quickly turned into a time of agony, uncertainty, fear, and confusion. Why would Christ, who knew how to multiply loaves and fishes for thousands, have sent them into such a vicious storm? Just hours ago, these same disciples were happily distributing loaves and fish to awestruck multitudes. Now, it seemed, they were about to be swallowed up by death itself.

Though we often see the difficulty we are in, sometimes we don't see the difficulty we *could* have been in if we had been left to ourselves. God may be preventing a greater trouble by allowing us to experience smaller ones. As difficult as being in this storm was, it was better for the disciples to be here than to be falling for the ideas of the crowd and seeking to turn Jesus away from His real mission. Who can tell how often God's people are hemmed in by trials for their own protection!

Omniscient Care

Scripture records another time when the disciples found themselves in a storm at sea, but then Christ had been with them in the boat (see Matt. 8:23–27). This time, Christ was not with them physically; however, He was with them spiritually. Though the disciples did not see Christ in the tempest on the lake, Mark tells us that *Christ* saw *them*: "And he saw them toiling in rowing" (6:48). This was supernatural sight, for through the darkness of the night, the distance, and the dreadful storm, no other human would have been able to see the ship with the disciples in it.

What a comfort this should be to believers! Perhaps you are in a place in life where you can't see the Lord. You're straining to see Him, but week in, week out, you're not able to catch a glimpse of His presence like you did in the past. When we lose sight of Him, it can be a great comfort that He doesn't lose sight of us (see Job 23:8–9). Although Jesus had been physically absent when the disciples struggled in their circumstances, His eyes were upon them all this time, and He ended up giving them a more magnificent view of His glory.

Magnificent Revelation

Matthew describes it this way: "And in the fourth watch [that is, about 3:00 a.m.] of the night Jesus went unto them, walking on the sea" (Matt. 14:25). Everything about Christ's coming to His disciples was so majestic—the timing, the manner, the direction. There was nothing hurried, harried, or hazardous about it. The picture the text paints is that He simply *willed* to be with His disciples, and no obstacle could stand in the way of that will.

Years later, as they wrote about that night, the disciples remembered their "hysterical shrieks" (that's what the phrase "cried out for fear" that Matthew used literally means) as they mistook Christ for a ghost or a phantom (Matt. 14:26; Mark 6:49–50). They thought they were doomed by the arrival of this being!

Why, with Jesus so near, would His disciples react like that? These men were exhausted after hours of rowing. If only they had seen by faith that the form they were so terrified of was actually their Savior coming with deliverance! Think of William Cowper's words:

> Ye fearful saints, fresh courage take;
> The clouds ye so much dread
> Are big with mercy, and shall break
> In blessings on your head.[7]

Christ called to the disciples across the water, and His words were filled with tender magnificence and magnificent tenderness: "Be of good cheer; it is I; be not afraid" (Matt. 14:27). Notice the three intricate parts of this statement, so filled with lessons: First, *He encouraged them*: "Be of good cheer." The literal meaning in the original is "take courage." Their courage had failed, and Christ tells them to take fresh courage.

Second, *He revealed Himself as God*. That was the reason they should take fresh courage. In the Old Testament, God gave His name to Moses as "I AM THAT I AM" (Ex. 3:14).

What Christ said here is short for exactly that. He means: "I am the faithful, covenant-keeping, immutable God who saves His people in distress. Amid everything that is topsy-turvy, I give stability and solidity." This self-revelation of Christ is the calm within their storm.

Third, *He consoled them*. The first part of Christ's words was a positive command. This last part is a negative command: "Be not afraid." It is as if He brought in courage and cast out fear, and all because He is the LORD.

Perhaps as you read this you are straining at the oars of life's storm. Making no headway is becoming tiresome. Perhaps it is even the fourth watch for you. Hear the One who says through His Word, "Take courage; it is I; be not afraid." In this divine "I" is the calm you need, the stronghold in the midst of the waves. What you need is to be centered on Him.

Centered Focus

Peter seems to have been the first to recognize Jesus, or at least the first one to dare to reply to Him. And certainly only Peter would dare to say, "Lord, if it be thou, bid me come unto thee on the water" (Matt. 14:28). Some Bible interpreters have disapproved of Peter for making this request, but Christ's answer was encouraging. "Come," Christ said, and "when Peter was come down out of the ship, he walked on the water" (Matt. 14:29). Peter entered by faith onto the solid surface that Christ's presence miraculously extended over the water.

But then something changed, and Peter felt himself sinking. He must have thought for a moment: "I'm going to drown after all!" But Christ was still there, still the I AM.

And so as Peter cried, "Lord, save me," we find that "immediately Jesus stretched forth his hand, and caught him" (Matt. 14:30–31). Peter, whose name means "stone," was held up by the solid Rock.

Notice that Jesus didn't rebuke Peter for having *no* faith, but He did rebuke him for being of "little faith" and for doubting (Matt. 14:31). That's one thing that the Holy Spirit teaches His people in the storms of life. The secret to stability in storms, you see, is a centered focus on Christ.

It is significant to read that Peter only *began* to sink (Matt. 14:30). The Lord didn't allow him to sink. Christ Himself on the cross would sink underneath the billows and waves of His Father's wrath in order that He might hold Peter up. He cried out in Psalm 69, a messianic psalm: "I sink in deep mire, where there is no standing; I am come into deep waters, where the floods overflow me" (v. 2). If you are outside of Christ, how will you stand when the floods of God's wrath come to swallow you up? You will be more terrified when you meet this Christ at last than these disciples who thought He was a ghost. Cry like Peter: "Lord, save me." He is able to save to the uttermost all who come unto God by Him (see Heb. 7:25).

We read, "The wind ceased" (Matt. 14:32). It had fulfilled its divine purpose. The trials God sends us are finished when they drive us into the arms of Christ in worship. The aim of them all is what we see when the disciples "worshipped Him, saying, Of a truth thou art the Son of God" (Matt. 14:33). Trials serve the glory of Christ. Why don't we glorify Him sooner? Lord, why do we need storms to bring us to our knees in adoration?

The account in John's gospel tells us that "immediately the ship was at the land whither they went" (6:21). It had taken hours to cover this distance. But with Christ on board, the next three miles were swiftly covered. What a picture of how the Lord's presence transforms life! With the Savior close, time passes quickly, until God's church reaches the other shore, where no storms can ever come, where she will never be between difficulties, but forever delivered.

Questions

1. For further study: you can read about this miracle in Mark 6:45–52 and John 6:14–21 also.

2. What does it mean that the Christian is "between deliverances"? Can a believer prepare for trials to come? If so, how?

3. What does this passage teach us about God's timing? What is the role of trust in this passage? Is it possible to exercise trust and patience in trials, and how?

4. Have you ever experienced storms in your life in which Christ seemed far away? What comfort can we draw from God's power displayed in this passage?

5. Jesus did not let Peter drown. What lesson did He teach Peter here? Why did Christ walk on the sea and not just calm the storm from a distance?

6. What does it mean when Jesus says, "Don't be afraid, it is I"? Is it realistic that Christ calls us not to fear in trials? What promise does this sentence give us?

7. Someone described Peter's problem as Christ "moving from the center of his eyes to the corner" and the storm moving from "the corner of his eyes to the center." Reflect on how that happens.

14

The Healing of the Daughter of a Canaanite Woman

Matthew 15:21–28

Jesus answered and said unto her, O woman, great is thy faith: be it unto thee even as thou wilt. And her daughter was made whole from that very hour.
—MATTHEW 15:28

In the late 1990s when I lived in Jerusalem for a while, I saw beggars daily at the gates of the city, holding out their hands. They all looked the same—pictures of need by the side of the road, taking what you put in their hands and giving a grateful nod. On one occasion, a friend and I passed some beggars near one of the gates. All of a sudden, we heard a cell phone go off. One of the beggars jumped up, pulled his phone out of his dingy bag, and walked away to answer it. We moved out of the way, watching. The "beggar's" demeanor had changed completely. He started arguing with the person to whom he was speaking and soon left the spot to hail a taxi. I was stunned until my friend explained that there are quite a few con artist beggars who dress the part and beg for money, even while they otherwise live normal lives in their apartments.

Unlike the beggar I saw that day, the woman we meet in Matthew 15 was a true beggar. She obtained a great and

gracious miracle from the Lord Jesus, namely, the healing of
her demon-possessed daughter.

A Needy Suppliant

In this passage, Christ was nearing the end of His Galilean
ministry. He had taught many things and done many miracles, and the time was soon approaching that He would leave
Galilee to go to Jerusalem. The opposition against Him had
been increasing as well, to the point that He determined to
withdraw to the northern edge of the Promised Land, into
the region of Tyre and Sidon. This area was the home of
many of the original Canaanites, whom Israel had been commanded to drive out of the Promised Land. God had often
sent judgments and curses on the Canaanites because of
their iniquity.

This region of Tyre and Sidon, however, had enjoyed
some tokens of favor in the past. Back in the days of King
David, Tyre's king, Hiram, had been allied with David and
provided wood from the forests of his region for building the
temple. Once, during a famine, the prophet Elijah had gone
to the region and miraculously supplied oil and meal for a
widow woman and her son to keep them alive.

Now another woman there needed help. We read that
this Canaanite woman came crying after Jesus, saying repeatedly, "O Lord, thou son of David; my daughter is grievously
vexed with a devil" (Matt. 15:22). The devil himself was
breathing down this woman's neck, it seemed. Satan had her
daughter in his grasp.

Notice that she called Jesus the "son of David." She
probably didn't know the Old Testament, but one of the

psalms had prophesied that the Son of David would "deliver the needy when he crieth; the poor also, and him that hath no helper" (Ps. 72:12). At any rate, it is clear that she had heard of Christ. Undoubtedly, she had heard of the many people who had been healed by Him, including those possessed by demons. Perhaps she had even heard how at one time He had spoken about her country when He had warned Chorazin and Bethsaida: "It shall be more tolerable for Tyre and Sidon... than for you.... For if the mighty works...done in you, had been done in Tyre and Sidon, they would have repented long ago in sackcloth and ashes" (Matt. 11:22, 21, respectively).

Clearly, the Holy Spirit had blessed whatever it was that she had heard so that she had counted it not simply as the word of men, but as the word of God (1 Thess. 2:13). And all the while, her need was so great. She was reminded every day of the devil's power over her daughter. Who could help her against such a powerful force?

A Trying Savior

We read of a number of trials that this needy woman encountered in her search for help. The first trial she encountered was the silence of Jesus. We read, "He answered her not a word" (Matt. 15:23). How discouraging to receive no answer at all to her cries. Perhaps it seemed to her that hell was open to her while heaven was closed to her—a demon-possessed daughter on the one hand, and a silent Savior on the other.

The second trial she encountered was the impatience of the disciples. This must have made matters worse for her. They even asked for Christ's help in getting rid of her: "Send her away; for she crieth after us" (Matt. 15:23).

The third trial this woman faced was the apparent rebuff of the Savior. When Christ finally did answer her, He seemed to push her away: "I am not sent but unto the lost sheep of the house of Israel" (Matt. 15:24). Her nationality was a strike against her she could do nothing about—she was a Canaanite. If only she had been an Israelite, one of the people among whom Christ had been walking! But Christ was no racist. He was simply explaining that His mission was focused on the nation of Israel, which was so lost at this time. In fact, as Christ would show, this woman would prove by her persistence and faith to be one of God's people. Christ is only bringing that into the light by His tests of her faith.

Note carefully the Savior's words here. He doesn't say, "I won't heal your daughter." He doesn't say, "I will not deal with you." So often we interpret silence as denial and discouragement as total rejection, but not this woman—she perseveres. After all, at first He was silent—and now she has gotten Him to speak. Though she does not yet have a positive answer, neither does she have an absolute denial. Though the door may not be opening for her yet, the door is still there, and He is still there behind the door, so why not keep knocking? Didn't He say elsewhere: "Ask, and it shall be given you; seek, and ye shall find; knock, and it shall be opened unto you" (Matt. 7:7)?

What was the Lord Jesus doing to this woman in these trials? Hadn't He Himself said: "All that the Father giveth me shall come to me; and him that cometh to me I will in no wise cast out" (John 6:37)? Indeed, the Lord would not cast this woman out. The all-wise Savior was putting her to the test to bring out the tenacity of her faith. He knew her faith before He tried her, just like the Lord knew Abraham's faith before He tried him (see Gen. 22:1).

The woman persisted despite the Savior's apparent rebuff. Kneeling down before Him, she spoke simply, yet strongly: "Lord, help me" (Matt. 15:25). In those three small words all her need was encapsulated. What a simple but clear glimpse into the heart of true prayer.

But the Lord was not done testing her. Now came her final, and arguably most severe, trial. Jesus said to her, "It is not meet to take the children's bread, and to cast it to dogs" (Matt. 15:26). Taken simply on the surface, this was an insult to the woman. It was as if He compared her to a yelping dog interrupting a father who was trying to feed his children.

It speaks to the woman's faith that she seems to have had her response ready. "Truth, Lord: yet the dogs eat of the crumbs which fall from their masters' table" (Matt. 15:27). If she had been offended by the Lord comparing her to an unclean animal, she would have missed the blessing the Lord was about to give her. But her eye was on one thing: the Lord's help. She knew how helpless and hopeless she was without it. As one author says, "Do not think God's delay is unwillingness; His willingness is infinite; His willingness is real; His seeming unwillingness is to make you do as the Canaanite woman did—persevere; His willingness waits to bestow more than we can ask or think. We must admit the truth of all that God says; and even from His frowns, His chastisements, His judgments, fetch new arguments, and point new appeals for mercy and forgiveness."[8] She was content to be called a dog. Like Jacob as he wrestled with God, this woman would not take no for an answer. Luther put it this way: "She wrung a Yea from God's Nay or to hear the deep-hidden Yea which many times lurks under His seeming Nay."[9]

A Rich Feast

The triumph of the woman could scarcely be greater. Not only was her daughter made whole from that very hour, but also Christ gave her so much more. He said to her, "Be it unto thee even as thou wilt" (Matt. 15:28). Though she was content with a crumb, the Savior put the whole of heaven's wealth at her disposal. The Lord could do this because, on the cross, His body would be broken and His blood shed for a full atonement. He could cast out this devil because He would defeat him at the cross. He could give this woman a rich feast because He hungered and thirsted under the displeasure of His Father for sinners such as her. In other words, He became a "worm, and no man" (Ps. 22:6) in order that outcasts such as this woman might be accepted as sons and daughters. He took her hell in order to make her an heir of heaven.

Perhaps you have had long nights of silence, discouragement after discouragement, or have even felt like hell was breathing down your neck. But while there is life, there is hope! This is the important question: Do you agree with what the Lord says about you in His Word? Do you agree that you are a dog, a leper, an outcast, and a rebel? Whatever He says, agree with Him quickly, wholeheartedly, for then the Lord will answer you as He did this woman: "Be it unto you even as you will."

Questions

1. For further study: you can read about this miracle in Mark 7:24–30 also.

2. Every Christian struggles with unanswered prayers, or the feeling of a closed heaven. How do you deal with your unanswered prayers, and how can you help others who feel that God does not hear?

3. How does the impatience of the disciples toward this woman convict us of our impatience at times with people who don't fit a certain mold? What should this tell us about how we regard those with needs around us?

4. Show how the woman's short prayer, "Lord, help me," had all the main ingredients of true prayer.

5. What do we learn from the woman about agreeing to what the Lord says about us in His Word? Why is that so difficult? Give an example of how this may have worked itself out in your life.

6. Was the healing of her daughter so small that it could be called a "crumb"? What does it say about her faith in God that she calls it a crumb? How does faith change our perspective of our circumstances and of God?

7. What does this chapter teach us about praying parents?

- 15 -

The Healing of the
Deaf-Mute Man

Mark 7:31–37

*And looking up to heaven, he sighed, and saith unto him…
Be opened. And straightway his ears were opened, and the
string of his tongue was loosed, and he spake plain.*

—MARK 7:34–35

Isaiah had prophesied regarding the time of Messiah: "Then
the eyes of the blind shall be opened, and the ears of the deaf
shall be unstopped. Then shall the lame man leap as an hart,
and the tongue of the dumb sing" (Isa. 35:5–6). During His
ministry Christ would fulfill this prophecy literally as well as
spiritually. In Mark 7, He healed a man who was both deaf
and, in effect, dumb, who stammered what were probably
mostly unintelligible sounds. Christ performed this miracle
for the sake of more than just this man. In these last days of
His ministry in Galilee, Christ was addressing the spiritual
condition of His disciples. Despite having been with Christ
so long, the disciples were still spiritually deaf, dumb, and
blind (Mark 6:52; 7:18; 8:17). Mark recounts a number of
physical healings that pictured what Christ could do spiritually. The miracle we will consider in this chapter was a sign of

the great spiritual transformation that would affect not only the disciples but untold multitudes after Pentecost.

The Prisoner of Silence

Just before He performed this miracle, Christ had been in the region of Tyre and Sidon (Mark 7:24, 31). After that, He went to Decapolis on the other side of the Sea of Galilee. He had been there before to free a man from a legion of demons (Mark 5:1–20). On that occasion the people had begged Him to leave (Mark 5:17), which He did. Now He had returned, and this time, somewhat unexpectedly, the people brought to the Lord Jesus a man described as being deaf and having an impediment in his speech.

The ability to speak is related to the ability to hear. When the latter is affected, the former suffers as well. Probably there had been a time when this man had been able to hear, at least a little. He was able to speak, but indistinctly or stammeringly. Today, sign language enables those who are hearing impaired to communicate at a fairly high level. In Bible times, however, one who was deaf was largely cut off from most forms of fellowship with others. He was, we might say, a prisoner of silence. Every sound directed his way was barred at his ears. Every sound coming from his mouth imploded into a garbled heap.

What a pitiful sight this was to the One whom Scripture calls the Word made flesh! When Christ descended to this earth, He came to a place ruined by the fall into sin. This man's physical plight was proof of the damage sin has wrought. In many ways he pictured the spiritual plight of Christ's disciples. Though they lived in close proximity to the

Savior, they lacked a basic understanding of Christ's heavenly origin and divine character. Despite all that Christ had said, they were still largely deaf to these things. Their speech was at best indistinct. Spiritually speaking, they weren't any better off than this deaf stammerer. What would transform them into apostles whose preaching and writing would reveal truth to great numbers of people? Their ears and mouths needed opening.

The Process of Restoration

The way Christ dealt with this man reflects the work He does when He restores a sinner to fellowship with Himself. Let's look at five aspects to this process.

First, the Lord Jesus dealt *personally* with this man. He took him "aside from the multitude" (Mark 7:33). When God works in our hearts, He does so in a way that isolates in order that we might have personal dealings with Him. That's what God did with Jacob when the angel wrestled with him at the Jabbok (Gen. 32:24). That's what God did with Saul of Tarsus when He dealt with him (Acts 9:8–9). That's what Christ did when He appeared to Peter after the resurrection (Luke 24:34). The same thing happened here. Christ did not perform this miracle in front of a large crowd, most of whom were only looking for something sensational. This miracle would be done under close wraps, with only the disciples and a few others as witnesses. Still today, there are many who would love to see an astounding miracle but would not be willing to receive instruction from it. Christ, however, won't cast this pearl before the masses, who are only looking for something dramatic.

Second, Christ dealt *intimately* with him. He "put his fingers into his ears, and he spit, and touched his tongue" (Mark 7:33). There were times when Christ healed from a distance or with a word. On this occasion, Christ was physically involved. It reminds us of how at the beginning God stooped down to breathe into Adam the breath of life, and he became a living soul (Gen. 2:7). Here, Christ's fingers touched the ears that were not functioning properly. He spit and touched the tongue that was not speaking properly. Christ actively took hold of this man, just as He actively took hold of our nature when He came to redeem lost people to Himself (Heb. 2:16).

We too need intimate dealings with Christ, in a spiritual sense. We need Him to point to the source of the problem in our lives that keeps us from hearing and heeding His word and that keeps us from praising and worshiping Him as we ought.

Third, Christ dealt with this man *looking heavenward*. Though this man couldn't hear, he could see. Is it possible that one of the last things he saw before his ears were opened and his tongue loosed was Christ "looking up to heaven" (Mark 7:34)? Christ's eyes directed this man's eyes upward. Christ Himself was already focused on His Father. A number of times, He specifically prayed before He performed a miracle (Mark 6:41; John 11:41–42). This time He spoke no words, yet His eyes were as a servant's upon his master (Ps. 123:2). Our only help is from the Lord, who made heaven and earth. What an encouragement it is to look upward in whatever need we have, physical or spiritual.

Fourth, Christ dealt with this man *sympathetically.* We read that the Savior "sighed" (Mark 7:34). We often sigh because of sin and the consequences of sin. Many of our prayers include sighs and groans, looking for the redemption of the body (Rom. 8:23). As the sympathizing High Priest, Christ knows such sighs. He utters them perfectly, as the One who can also supply perfectly for each needy sigh. But it is not without travail for the Savior. When Christ healed the woman with the issue of blood, "virtue" went out of Him (Mark 5:30). When Christ was at the grave of Lazarus, He groaned in Himself (John 11:38). Christ gave Himself trouble, so to speak, in order to reverse the consequences of the fall. In the process, He Himself "bare our sicknesses" (Matt. 8:17), and because of Calvary, His sighs and those of His people are heard in heaven.

Fifth, Christ dealt with this man *authoritatively.* We read that Christ gave a strong command. Mark notes that He gave it in the Aramaic language that was spoken in this area: "Ephphatha," meaning, "Be opened" (Mark 7:34). Though this man could not hear, Christ remarkably directed the order to the man, and this is the first word he heard— straight from the mouth of the Savior. What a word it was! It was the one word that opened the way for him to hear and speak thousands of other words.

The Praise for the Redeemer

Literally, the text says, "The chain of his tongue was loosed" (Mark 7:35). What a special sign Christ had performed! The prisoner of silence was now freed. He could hear and speak through the power of a Redeemer who opened His ears and loosed His tongue. One word from the Savior, and this man's chain fell off. He was free!

The restoration was immediate and effective. We read that the man "spake plain" (Mark 7:35). He did not have to go through a process of learning how to put sounds and syllables together to make words and sentenced. His tongue could now glorify God as it had been created to do.

Christ's "Ephphatha" still opens spiritual prisons today. Years later, for example, the Lord spoke from heaven when He opened the heart of Lydia. As a result of Christ's opening work in her life, she "attended unto the things which were spoken of Paul" (Acts 16:14). From that moment, Lydia heard and spoke like she never had before. All disciples in every age need this almighty "Ephphatha." Their spiritual eyes, mouths, and hearts need to be opened.

It is no wonder that this narrative ends in a chorus of praise. Even though Christ forbade that the miracle be broadcast far and wide, its effect reverberated over the countryside of Decapolis: "He hath done all things well," the astonished witnesses of this miracle said (Mark 7:37). Similar praise has been heard throughout the ages everywhere this Redeemer speaks a spiritual "Ephphatha." By His word and Spirit, spiritual prisons are still unlocked today. After all, He is the Word made flesh.

Questions

1. Survey the ways in which this deaf stammerer is similar to the disciples at this point in Christ's ministry, spiritually speaking. How will things change for Peter by Mark 8:29 and then by Acts 2:14?

2. The last time we read of Decapolis, the people begged the Savior to leave (Mark 5:17). Now things appear to have changed to some degree. How does this encourage us regarding the Savior?

3. How is what Jesus did to this deaf stammerer similar to what we read in John 20:22? How does He do this in the lives of people whom He is changing today?

4. Think of how hands-on this miracle was. What does this tell us about the Savior? Why do you think Christ sighed as He said, "Ephphatha"?

5. Begin to think of *all* the things that Christ has done well. Write some of them down.

16

Healing in Stages

Mark 8:22-26

After that he put his hands again upon his eyes, and made him look up: and he was restored, and saw every man clearly.
—MARK 8:25

During His ministry Christ restored sight to many blind people (see, e.g., Matt. 9:27–31; 11:5; 15:30; John 9:1–3). As we saw at the beginning of the previous chapter, this is something that the prophet Isaiah had foretold: "Then the eyes of the blind shall be opened" (Isa. 35:5). This prophecy would find both literal and spiritual fulfillment.

Spiritual sight is the focus of this miracle in Mark 8. Mark is the only gospel writer who records this event. The context makes clear that the disciples' ideas of who Christ was were impoverished. In the previous chapter Christ lamented: "Are ye so without understanding also? Do ye not perceive…?" (v. 18). Also in this chapter Christ probed them: "Perceive ye not yet, neither understand?" (v. 17).

We know what it is like in everyday life to transition suddenly from complete darkness to bright light. Imagine being in a dark room with the shades drawn and the lights out. You stumble to open the door and leave the room. You then find yourself in a room bright with light both from the lamps in the room and the bright sunlight reflecting off freshly fallen snow and streaming in through the window. Your eyes would need time to adjust to such a change. Because His disciples needed time to "adjust," Christ didn't give them a full sight of Himself all at once, but rather showed them glimpses of His glory. Let's consider this process in the healing of the blind man.

Seeing Nothing

This miracle took place outside the city of Bethsaida, near where Christ had multiplied the loaves for the five thousand. This was on the east side of the Sea of Galilee, close to the spot where the Jordan River flows into the lake. Christ had withdrawn to this place as He was preparing for His suffering and death at Jerusalem. But people heard of His whereabouts, and a blind man was brought to Him for healing. Mark 8:22 tells us that those who brought him asked that Christ "touch him."

Physical blindness is a real and painful disability for many people in our world. But how many more are afflicted with spiritual blindness? There are millions in our world who have scarcely seen the inside of a church building. There are others who "feel their way" to church each week and warm their pews and do their part in the externals of worship. And yet they are blind to the beauty of Christ, the glory of God, and their need for the Spirit's work. The cross of Christ means nothing to them; the hereafter is a foggy concept. What is the cure for such devastating blindness?

The only cure is to be taken aside as Christ did to the man who was dumb and mute (Mark 7:32) in the previous chapter and the blind man here in Mark 8. Many "miracle workers" today want to do their "wonders" in front of large groups of people on stages and on television programs broadcast around the world. But Christ was not seeking applause or fame. He would not have His miracle be a distraction, nor did He want to engender feverish excitement. His goal was to reach where no one could see—into the heart. He would work quietly, unobserved by fickle, flighty multitudes.

Seeing Men as Trees, Walking

Christ could have worked an immediate cure for this man. However, Christ wanted to use this miracle to teach His disciples how He often gives spiritual sight gradually. So He took the man and led him out of the town (Mark 8:23). The way in which Christ performed the miracle told a story.

First, *Jesus spat on the blind man's eyes* (Mark 8:23a). Why would He do this? We know that He used this means on other occasions (see Mark 7:33; John 9:6), but we can't be sure why. It certainly proves this: what may first seem reprehensible to us may serve our great good. God can use the Bible that unbelievers despise to save them. He uses the foolishness of preaching to save people. The cross, a shameful symbol from which we might turn away, becomes a means of life and salvation. God's power is glorified through such means.

Second, *Christ put His hands on him* (Mark 8:23b). He had likely already touched him when He had led him out of town. Now He probably touched the man's eyes. Touch was a form of communication that was undoubtedly important to this man. Christ's touching the man's blind eyes would also have been a visible identification of the man's problem. The Lord does the same thing, spiritually, when He convicts us of our sin. By His word He puts His finger, as it were, right on the problem.

Third, *Christ asked a searching question* (Mark 8:23c). We read, "He asked him if he saw ought." He didn't ask the man how he felt. He didn't ask him if he had experienced anything. He didn't ask him for his opinions. He asked him if he *saw*. This was the real test. The true test of whether the Lord has done a work on us is this: Have our spiritual eyes been opened? Can we see our guilt? Can we see His glory? Can we see His mercy? What is your answer to Christ's question? Have the scales fallen off your eyes?

Now it is worth noting that Christ didn't ask him simply whether he saw, but whether he saw "ought," that is, anything. Christ, of course, knew exactly what He was doing. But for the sake of the disciples, Christ wanted this man to express what had happened, and this man used an interesting word picture: "I see men as trees, walking" (Mark 8:24). In other words, his sight was not yet clear. Except for the fact that people walked and trees didn't, he wouldn't have been able to tell them apart yet.

What an honest answer this man gave! If he had pretended he could see perfectly, he would soon have proved himself to be a real fool. All upon whom the Lord works still have imperfect and incomplete views of reality. They see, but not clearly. They are apt to confuse things, especially at first. But when the Lord's work has an effect, as with this man, we acknowledge it. We desire to see more and understand more.

How important it is not to despise the day of small things (see Zech. 4:10). But, it is also important not to be content with half sight. Tell the Master honestly that you still see and understand so little. Those who are content with vague notions should examine whether Christ has even worked upon them.

Seeing Clearly

Notice that Christ did not take more drastic measures than He had used previously in order to complete this man's cure. We read: "After that he put his hands again upon his eyes." He essentially only repeated what He had done before, until the man was fully "restored, and saw every man clearly" (Mark 8:25). Nothing else was needed.

So too, God often heals our blindness through the repeated use of the means of grace, especially the preaching of His word, blessed by the Holy Spirit. He does it in steps and stages, as He did when He created the world. This does not mean at all that Christ's power was limited. What He could have done in one moment at the beginning of creation, He used six days to do. So too, He re-creates His people, step by step, asking them again and again to own the work He has done in their hearts. This is His chosen way of revealing Himself to sinners.

When the man was fully healed, we are told that he "saw...clearly" (Mark 8:25). The word in the original is a combination of two words that together literally mean "radiantly into the distance." What a beautiful and descriptive phrase! Truly, Christ brings His people to see things far off as if they were close (Heb. 11:7, 13).

It is not coincidental that right after this miracle, Peter confessed that Jesus is the Christ (Mark 8:27–29). This was a breakthrough moment for Peter. Still, however, he and the others had only a vague understanding of who Christ was and what He came to do. Just as He did with this man whom He was healing, Christ had His hands on their spiritual eyes, and He would make their sight clearer and clearer.

Though Christ was teaching His disciples through this miracle, there was a profound benefit for this man, and not just a physical one. Now that the man could see clearly, Christ sent him away to his house rather than into town (Mark 8:26). The last thing this man needed was, as we would say today, to sign a book deal. This sensational world has no eye for Christ. Christ would save him from the instantaneous fame he might attract. When the Lord gives this gift of new spiritual sight to you, it is better to test, appreciate, and use your newfound sight in your family and previous station than to have the big crowd claim you as its own.

Questions

1. The people bring their blind friend to Jesus. What do they recognize, and how is this an example for us?

2. Why did Christ take this man out of the city, and how might He do that today?

3. If I am content with my current knowledge of my sin and of Christ, what does that mean? Why?

4. What is the significance of this miracle as it relates to Mark 7:18; 8:17; and 8:29?

5. What are some of the "faraway things" that the Bible says that those who have spiritual sight see (see, e.g., Eph. 1:18–19; Heb. 11:1, 7, 13, 27)?

6. Why did Christ tell the man not to broadcast this miracle in the city (Mark 8:26)? How does this truth apply spiritually?

17

The Healing of the Boy at the Foot of the Mountain

Mark 9:14–29

Jesus said unto him, If thou canst believe, all things are possible to him that believeth. And straightway the father of the child cried out, and said with tears, Lord, I believe; help thou mine unbelief.

—MARK 9:23–24

The glory of Christ seems such an otherworldly concept that we, earthbound creatures that we are, cannot wrap our minds around it. How can such a glorious Christ, who dwells in majesty on high, stoop low enough to meet us, His creatures, in our need and sin and emptiness? When we think of His glorious transfiguration in the presence of three of His disciples, we wonder how human eyes could have even taken in such a sight. We could never, we might think, be able to be witnesses of such glory!

And yet Christ showed Himself no less of a glorious Lord after His descent from the Mount of Transfiguration. For shortly thereafter, He performed an amazing miracle, a testimony of the glory He is willing to reveal to poor and needy sinners.

The Glorious Christ Descends to the Valley

Mark 9 begins on a geographical and spiritual high note. Christ took three of His disciples (Peter, James, and John) to a high mountain. This mountain became a holy and heavenly place as Christ was transfigured there, before the disciples' eyes (9:2). His garments glistened radiantly, "shining" and "exceeding white." Moses and Elijah, two Old Testament saints who had gone to glory in heaven, now came and talked with Christ on this mountain (9:3–4). What a majestic scene! It would have been understandable if the disciples had feared that they would be consumed in light of such an event. No wonder that "they were sore afraid" (9:6)! They must have been even more amazed when they heard the voice of the Father from an overshadowing cloud: "This is my beloved Son: hear him" (9:7). But rather than staying on the mountain to be worshiped there by His disciples, as Peter suggested (9:5), Christ had the great work of redemption to complete, and nothing would take Him away from that work.

What would be the first sight of the "real world" that would greet the descending Lord and His three disciples? One can't help thinking about how, during their lifetimes, both Moses and Elijah had also had "mountaintop experiences"—Moses on Mount Sinai and Elijah on Mount Carmel. Upon their descent from those mountains, both men had soon met the harsh realities of a sinful world and of sinful people. Moses had come down from receiving God's sacred commandments only to be confronted with the idolatry of the children of Israel. His anger at this sin led him to break the tables of stone (Ex. 32:19). And Elijah had come down from the glorious display of the God of Israel's power on Mount Carmel only to have his life threatened by the wicked and revengeful Queen Jezebel. He had fled to Beer-sheba (1 Kings 19:1–3).

When Christ came down from the Mount of Transfiguration, He was met with something even more sinister than the realities of a sinful world and of sinful people—He was met by the devil himself! As He came down to His other disciples, He saw a great multitude around them (Mark 9:14). Among the people who had gathered was the father of a demon-possessed boy who came forward to describe his predicament to the Lord Jesus.

We know several details about this suffering boy. He was an only child (Luke 9:38) who had probably suffered in this way for years, since childhood (Mark 9:21). The gospel writer Matthew tells us that he was a "lunatick" (17:15). A number of symptoms the gospel writers mention are consistent with what we know today as epileptic seizures. Mark tells us that in addition, however, this boy was both deaf and dumb (9:17, 25). And, most significantly, a demon had taken hold of him (9:17, 18, 25). This evil spirit had often tried to drown the boy in water or burn him in fire (9:22). No wonder, then, that Matthew describes him as "sore vexed," or, as it literally reads, "he suffers miserably" (17:15). What an accurate description of the effect the devil has on us! He comes to steal, to kill, and to destroy (John 10:10).

In his great need, this man had come seeking the right Person. In Christ's absence, however, the disciples at the base of the mountain had tried to help the boy, but they had been powerless to do anything. In fact, scribes had interfered, arguing with them (Mark 9:14, 16). The impression that we get is that here, at the foot of the mountain, there had been lots of arguing, but little action; lots of words, but little work being accomplished. Isn't this so typical when we are faced with problems too difficult for us? Well-meaning disciples of Christ are powerless in the face of what Christ alone can do. How often do believers occupy themselves with arguing and debating instead of walking worthy of their calling!

What a drastic change of scene for the Savior! On the mountain He had been near, as it were, to the gate of heaven. Now He stood as if at the door of hell. On the mountain He had spoken with Moses and Elijah about the work of redemption, which He would accomplish (Luke 9:31); this boy would now become an object lesson of what His work would involve. Christ would show by His actions what redeeming miserable captives of Satan looks like. And, not long after this event, Christ would Himself enter into the forsakenness of hell, bearing the curse and punishment His people deserve as part of His redemptive work. What a condescending Savior! He not only displays His glory on the mountaintops but also in the valleys in the presence of the forces of evil.

The Glorious Christ Nurtures Faith

It is interesting and instructive to notice that before conquering the forces of darkness present in the spectacle before Him here, Christ first addressed issues of the heart. In other words, before performing a visible miracle, Christ worked in an invisible realm, teaching about faith and encouraging its growth and development. This is a very important part of Christ's work.

He first spoke an honest word of rebuke: "O faithless generation, how long shall I be with you? how long shall I suffer you?" (Mark 9:19). This rebuke was aimed at the multitude

in general but also at the disciples and the father, and it targeted the unbelief in their hearts. Why would the Lord speak
this way? His words may seem harsh, especially in light of the
well-meaning disciples and a grieving father. But we should
not be surprised if Christ wounds before He heals. He acted
here as a good surgeon would, using the knife to get to the
root of the problem of unbelief. How great an evil unbelief
is! It is greater in magnitude, even, than the devil's hold on
this boy was. Let us search our own hearts on this matter.
What would the Lord say of our hearts? Is there unbelief to
be found there? Does He have cause to lament over us the
way He did over the people gathered here in this chapter?

After rebuking the unbelief in the hearts of those present,
Christ went on to nurture the faith in the heart of the boy's
father. He called for the boy to be brought to Him (Mark
9:19). He first asked the father, "How long is it ago since this
came unto him?" (Mark 9:21). The father answered that the
boy had been afflicted with this demon since childhood.

No wonder, then, that the man implored: "If thou canst
do any thing, have compassion on us, and help us" (Mark
9:22). And yet his first word is "if"! This word betrayed the
weakness of the man's faith, the doubt that was in his heart
about whether Christ could be of any help to his son.

Christ proceeded by taking straight aim at this "if." He
said to the man, "If thou canst believe, all things are possible to him that believeth" (Mark 9:23). The original Greek
draws attention to the word "if," literally saying, "Regarding
the 'if,' if *you* believe..." Christ's point was that this man was
putting his "if" in the wrong place. The question was not
whether *Christ could do* what this man wanted; the question
was whether *the man believed that Christ could do* it.

A note of caution is appropriate. The Lord Jesus was not saying here that a person possessing faith can necessarily receive a miracle. Many people twist the meaning of this and other passages of Scripture to support their belief in faith miracles. It is as if they can just think their way to a miracle by positive, upbeat thinking. But genuine faith goes even further than a belief in miracles. Miraculous faith might think it can believe enough to bring about a miracle. But true faith believes more and trusts more than that, for even when our hoped-for miracle doesn't happen or is delayed, true faith doesn't stop. It believes all things. It hopes all things. It was through a true faith like this that the apostle Paul could live with the thorn in his flesh, even after praying repeatedly that God would remove it, for God would supply His sufficient grace (2 Cor. 12:9). Even if a desired request is not granted the way that faith wants it to be, as Christ said, "*All* things are possible to him that believeth."

The faith lesson that Christ was teaching here was a most precious one. This is at the heart of how Christ brings His glory to bear on miserable sinners such as you and me. He calls forth faith. He refines faith. He works through faith. He gives faith as an empty hand to receive all things from Him. Through faith, the glorious Christ reveals His glory. He doesn't entrust His glory to anything else. Faith alone as the gift of God will receive His glory.

In response to the glorious revelation of Christ to his heart, this man went on to evidence true faith, in its weakness but also in all its strength and its reality. Crying out, he confessed: "Lord, I believe; help thou mine unbelief" (Mark 9:24). Under the glorious gaze of Christ, he admitted both his faith and his unbelief. Notice, however, how he spoke first from the perspective of faith: "I believe." Then, in the next breath, he begged for Christ's assistance. He needed help, not because of the devil who was possessing his child, but because of a greater foe: the unbelief in his heart.

The Glorious Christ Rewards Faith

The greater battle—the one in the father's heart—was won. The smaller battle would also be quickly resolved. We read in Mark 9:25: "When Jesus saw that the people came running together, he rebuked the foul spirit, saying unto him, Thou dumb and deaf spirit, I charge thee, come out of him, and enter no more into him." Despite the violent, hellish response of the demon, who cried and rent the boy sore, Christ's simple, decisive command was all that was needed to effect the boy's complete cure. Hell cannot stand before the glory of heaven. Even when it appeared to the people that the boy was "as one dead," the glorious Christ simply "took him by the hand, and lifted him up; and he arose" (Mark 9:26–27).

What a miraculous, visible demonstration of Christ's power was given to the multitude gathered at the foot of the mountain that day! What an illustration of what Christ's incarnation, suffering, death, and resurrection would accomplish. He came from heaven to free a captive and miserable people bent on their own destruction. Still today He calls forth faith in Himself and nurtures it, even in afflicted, tried, and assaulted souls, and that for His glory.

Questions

1. For further study: you can read about this miracle in Matthew 17:14–21 and Luke 9:37–42 also.

2. There are many contrasts between this miracle and the glorious scene on the Mount of Transfiguration that precedes it. Name a few of them, and show how they capture Christ's mission from heaven to this earth. What does this tell us about God's grace?

3. Name a need in your life that drives you to the Savior. Does God change our needs when we live closer to Him? Trace how we see this principle displayed in the father.

4. What does this passage tell us about the importance of believing while asking of God? Why might this be so important to God before He works in our lives?

5. How was the man's cry, "Help thou mine unbelief," already evidence of the presence of true faith? Do you ever feel that unbelief stands between you and God's promises? What does this passage teach us about this?

6. Name some of the things in this passage that Christ uses to demonstrate His attributes. Give some examples of how He shows the same things today.

7. What can you learn from Christ first dealing with the heart of the man before He saved the child's life?

18

The Coin in the Fish's Mouth

Matthew 17:24–27

> *Go thou to the sea, and cast an hook, and take up the fish*
> *that first cometh up; and when thou hast opened his mouth,*
> *thou shalt find a piece of money.*
> —MATTHEW 17:27

The miracle of the coin in the fish's mouth probably took place about six months before Christ's crucifixion. The disciple Peter plays a central role in this narrative. Peter, who had been taught by the Spirit of God, had already confessed that Christ was the Son of God—we read about this in Matthew 16:16. But there was more that Peter had to learn, both about himself and about Christ. As we look at this narrative and miracle, let's focus on how the Lord Jesus reveals Himself to Peter in four ways.

An All-Wise Prophet

While he was with Jesus and the other disciples in Capernaum, Peter was approached by tax collectors, who asked him, "Doth not your master pay tribute?" (Matt. 17:24). The tribute to which these men were referring was not a civil/governmental tax, but a religious, or ecclesiastical, tax. It was also referred to as the "temple tax." The payment for this tax was a coin known as a *didrachma*, which would be equivalent to a day laborer's wages for two days of work. Temple taxes originated back in Old Testament times. We read already in Exodus of every adult Israelite male being required to pay half a shekel as "ransom money." We're not sure whether this was to be an annual tax or whether it was a one-time tax, a collection of sorts for the building of the tabernacle (Ex. 35:21–29; 38:25–31). Later, a similar tax was levied for the rebuilding of the temple during Nehemiah's time (Neh. 10:32–33). At any rate, in New Testament times the temple tax was collected annually.

The tax collectors who approached Peter obviously thought of him as a spokesperson for the Lord Jesus. And Peter did speak for Him, albeit rather thoughtlessly. He answers them, "Yes." But when Peter mentioned the conversation to Jesus later, the Lord Jesus "prevented [or, anticipated] him," thereby showing His omniscience (Matt. 17:25). Although he had not been present with Peter at the time, he knew all Peter's thoughts and words perfectly. He is the silent witness to our every conversation. And so Jesus succinctly and perceptively posed this question of Peter: "What thinkest thou, Simon? of whom do the kings of the earth take custom or tribute? of their own children, or of strangers?" (Matt. 17:25). In other words, Jesus said to Peter, "Earthly kings don't collect tax money from their family members—they require taxes of their subjects." Jesus was reminding Peter of His kingly Sonship. "I am," He was saying, "the Son of the heavenly King. Do I need to pay taxes?"

We don't know exactly why Peter had answered the tax collectors as he did. He may not have given the question much thought. Perhaps he felt pressure to answer as he did, wanting to please. Whatever the reason, let's not fail to see the poignancy of Jesus' question to Peter. Remember, this is Peter, the disciple who had just confessed Christ's royal Sonship when he said, "Thou art the Christ, the Son of the living God" (Matt. 16:16). Had he forgotten about his master's Lordship when he agreed with the tax collectors?

How often do professing Christians do the same thing? It's not a coincidence that Jesus used Peter's old name, "Simon" (Matt. 17:25). Peter acted so easily and quickly in line with his old nature. How God's people need so much more renewing of their minds (Rom. 12:2)! It is no wonder that Christ asked Peter, "What thinkest thou?" or, "What are you thinking?" What a mercy it is that the Lord is such a patient teacher.

We should also notice here that if we are professing Christians, all our actions project upon our Lord and Master. By his quick "yes," Peter had detracted from His Master's honor. In essence, he had added to His humiliation by allowing Jesus to be portrayed as less than God. Let us take a lesson from this. It's really either/or: either we magnify the Lord in what we say, do, and think, or we diminish His glory. May the Lord forgive us for doing the latter so often and so unthinkingly.

A Humble Servant

It is amazing to see how willingly Christ submitted Himself to this temple ordinance, allowing Himself to be seen as a subject rather than the Son of God. He who had proclaimed

Himself to be "greater than the temple" (Matt. 12:6) was willing, His divine person notwithstanding, to submit Himself to a temple ordinance. Even as He was Lord over all, even over the temple, He was willing, in the words of Paul, to make "himself of no reputation," taking "the form of a servant" (Phil. 2:7). And so He would stoop here to pay this earthly tax like everyone else around Him.

Notice, however, the reason Jesus gave for His paying the tax: "lest we should offend them" (Matt. 17:27). Peter's reasoning had not seemed to be along this line. But Christ's heart was such that He would forego His rights in order to serve the good of others, as Paul would later instruct Christians to do (Rom. 14:21; 1 Cor. 8:13; Gal. 5:13). Christ came not to do His own will, but the will of His Father (John 6:38) and to seek and to save the lost (Luke 19:10).

The lesson for us is obvious. If the Son of God did not insist on His rights, but gave them up so as not to put a stumbling block before ignorant sinners, how can we insist on our rights and thereby make others stumble? "Owe no man any thing, but to love one another" (Rom. 13:8). There are Christians who flaunt their "royal rights" before the world with an independent and arrogant spirit, giving reason for the gospel to be spoken of in an evil way. It should not be so with the child of God who has learned to follow his Master in lowliness of mind, esteeming others better than himself.

An Omnipotent Lord

For Peter's further instruction, Christ commanded him to go "to the sea, and cast an hook, and take up the fish that first cometh up; and when thou hast opened his mouth,

thou shalt find a piece of money" (Matt. 17:27). Though it
is not recorded what happened when Peter obeyed his Master, there can be no doubt that Christ's word was fulfilled
exactly as He spoke it. This miracle proved the Lord's *omniscience* and *omnipotence*. Christ spoke to Peter with such calm
confidence. He knew of a fish in the water with a coin in its
mouth, and this fish would be the first one to come to Peter's
hook. Surely, He is a free Son of the Lord of lords. He is
the Creator Himself. He is the One who was in the "world,
and the world was made by him, and [yet] the world knew
him not" (John 1:10). "In his hand are the deep places of the
earth.... The sea is his, and he made it" (Ps. 95:4–5).

Can Christ, then, not discern your need, child of God?
And if the Lord could provide in this need, would He not
know how to provide in your need? He is at no loss to provide for us, temporally or eternally, since truly, nothing is too
hard for the Lord (Gen. 18:14).

A Redeeming Savior

There is even more to this rich miracle. The coin that Peter
would find in the fish would be twice what was needed for
Christ alone. The Greek word for the coin is *stater*, which is
twice as much as a *didrachma*. So Christ says: "That take, and
give unto them for me and thee" (Matt. 17:27).

What a beautiful picture of how Christ would pay for
Peter in a spiritual way! Even though Peter might have been
able to pay this particular debt, Christ wanted him to know
that He, as the Lord of heaven, had stooped so low in order
to pay the price for the sins of people such as Peter so that
their spiritual debts might be paid in full. Christ would

become poor that through His poverty Peter might become rich (2 Cor. 8:9).

Peter would write later about this redeeming work of His Lord and Savior: "Forasmuch as ye know that ye were not redeemed with corruptible things, as silver and gold, from your vain conversation received by tradition from your fathers; but with the precious blood of Christ, as of a lamb without blemish and without spot" (1 Peter 1:18–19).

Remember that, according to Exodus 30:12, this kind of tax was originally designated to be ransom money. This gives added significance to the Lord's payment for Peter. Before God, Peter could never have paid his own ransom price, much less the price for anyone else. Psalm 49 explains: "None of them can by any means redeem his brother, nor give to God a ransom for him" (v. 7). Yet as the One greater than the temple, Christ could, for He had come "to give his life a ransom for many" (Matt. 20:28).

Not only would Christ pay the ransom price for Peter, He would also make Him a free child of the King. In Matthew 17:26, Christ had spoken in the plural: "Then are the children free." Because of Christ's finished work, Peter was now both a child of God and an heir of heaven (see Rom. 8:17). Christ, the firstborn Son of God, had become a servant and purchased these rights for Peter. In 1 Corinthians 3:21–22, Christ told the church of Corinth that Peter was theirs: "All things are yours, whether Paul, or Apollos, or Cephas [that is, Peter]." Peter was no longer his own. He had been bought with a costly price (see 1 Cor. 6:19–20), and he was now going to be a servant of the church of Jesus Christ.

Questions

1. Think of a time when you quickly agreed to something and later realized your decision, even though well intentioned, was not the best. How does Romans 12:2 address this?

2. Christ knew Peter's thoughts before he even uttered them. In fact, He discerned Peter's thinking better than Peter did. How might we live differently if Psalm 139:23–24 were our daily prayer?

3. Give a practical example of how Christians should not insist on their rights when it would offend others. How does this passage show that our motives for doing something are important?

4. What are a number of things we learn about Christ from this miracle? How do they apply to your life?

5. In what ways are Christians "free" (Matt. 17:26)? You might find the Westminster Confession of Faith, chapter 20, helpful. How should Christians handle governmental policies that we do not agree with?

6. Probably this miracle put Peter in his proper place. Reflect on what Peter may have learned about himself and how God might teach us similarly in everyday events in our lives.

19

The Woman with the Bent Back

Luke 13:10–17

> *And when Jesus saw her, he called her to him, and said unto her, Woman, thou art loosed from thine infirmity. And he laid his hands on her: and immediately she was made straight, and glorified God.*
>
> —LUKE 13:12–13

What a blessing it is to have a day of rest! After creating all things by the word of His power, God sanctified the seventh day so that His creation would rest in worshiping Him (Gen. 2:3). God affirmed the institution of the Sabbath at Sinai when He wrote with His own finger these words: "Remember the sabbath day, to keep it holy" (Ex. 20:8).

The day of rest should not be a day chiefly of rules and regulations; that is how the Pharisees corrupted the Sabbath. In contrast, Christ used the Sabbath to worship God in His appointed means and to do many works of mercy so that people would rest in Him, His mercy, and His finished work. Among other things, this is what He was teaching in His miracle involving the woman with the bent back.

The Infirm Woman

In the time leading up to this incident, Christ had begun to go to Jerusalem (Luke 9:51) and was traveling one last time through Perea on the other side of the Jordan. In the passage we are considering, He was in a synagogue for the last recorded time during His earthly ministry.

Luke suddenly introduces us to one of the congregants that Sabbath day: "And, behold, there was a woman which had a spirit of infirmity eighteen years, and was bowed together" (13:11). In the surrounding verses, we are told three things about her condition.

First, her frame was completely pulled together. It wasn't that her back was bent only slightly, but, as the original says, bent together, or completely bent over. She had been this way for eighteen years. She couldn't look up into the sky or into people's faces. She was so disfigured that she was likely teased and mocked by children as she made her difficult way through life.

The spiritual parallel becomes clear when we see, *second, that this woman had been bound by Satan.* In verse 16, Christ tells us that Satan had bound this woman eighteen years ago. She had a "spirit of infirmity" (Luke 13:11). Luke, a medical doctor, specifically mentions this. In other words, she did not simply have a physical condition involving a misaligned spine. This was both a medical and spiritual problem. The devil had bound her so that she shuffled around every day as if chained by him.

Third, this woman could do nothing to help herself. Luke 13:11 reiterates this: "and could in no wise lift up herself." How amazing, then, that we meet this woman in the

synagogue. She puts to shame anyone looking for an easy
excuse to stay away from church. Despite her pain and the
shame she might have felt, her feet shuffled down the cob-
bled streets of this town until she reached the place where
she could hear the Word of God read and explained. On this
particular Sabbath, Christ was the preacher, anointed from
heaven "to proclaim liberty to the captives, and the opening
of the prison to them that are bound" (Isa. 61:1).

The Restoring Physician

This woman with the bent back could probably not have seen
the preacher that day, but He saw her. Luke tells us that this
Physician did three things to His patient.

First, He looked at her. "Jesus saw her" (13:12). This
emphasizes the one-sided work of God's grace. Many others came to Jesus asking for healing; this woman may also
have prayed to the Lord many times for healing. But here,
the Lord Jesus saw her in a way that no one else can see. He
saw her as the Lord saw His people tormented in bondage
in Egypt when He told Moses, "I have surely seen the afflic-
tion of my people" (Ex. 3:7). His was not a casual look, but a
compassionate one.

Second, He called her to Him (13:12). She likely couldn't
see Christ, but, shuffling all the way, she followed His voice
until she came to Him. Christ's call was powerful and effectual in her life. "My sheep hear my voice," He says in John
10:27. With her in His presence, He issued the call of liberty
from bondage: "Woman, thou art loosed from thine infirmity"
(13:12). Notice how there was no uncertainty in His words

or demeanor. He didn't even command; he simply stated the fact—but what a transformation was contained in it.

Third, He touched her (13:13). Under His touch, the spirit of infirmity left, the devil gave way, and this woman was no longer crushed, but stood upright. Now she could look up at the sun and into people's faces! And she could see her Great Physician's face. This synagogue had never seen the likes of such a miracle. Christ's words were effectual for a complete cure for the woman.

The Lord is pleased to do this same spiritual miracle in the life of every one of His children. When sinners are burdened with sin and its guilt and under the curse of the law, God does for them what He did for Israel in Leviticus 26:13: "I have broken the bands of your yoke, and made you go upright." This spiritual freedom is possible only because Christ would soon be bound and delivered up to be crucified. Because He was bound, His people can go free (John 18:8–12).

Have you experienced the freedom of your spiritual chains falling off? Has the burden of your sin and transgression rolled away because of the look, word, and touch of Christ through the Spirit? If it has, you will do the same thing this woman did, namely, glorify God (Luke 13:13). We can't claim to be changed by Christ if our lives are not fundamentally oriented to the praise and glory of a gracious God. The Lord Himself said, "This people have I formed for myself; they shall shew forth my praise" (Isa. 43:21).

The Instructing Lord

The narrative doesn't end with the healing of the woman. As the woman was glorifying God, something sinister took place. "The ruler of the synagogue answered with indignation, because that Jesus had healed on the sabbath day, and said unto the people, There are six days in which men ought to work: in them therefore come and be healed, and not on the sabbath day" (Luke 13:14). Clearly, the glory of God was not on the mind of this man. Thinking himself wiser than the Lord of the Sabbath (see Matt. 12:8), he accused the Great Physician of breaking the Sabbath.

Why did this man react so vehemently to this healing? He reacted this way because every time the devil is forced to relinquish some of his prey, he tries to strike back. But there was more going on here. What made this man so indignant? He seemed to have had far less of a problem watching this woman suffer than seeing her healed. What kind of spirit would respond like this? His remark is proof that his own spirit was even more in bondage than this woman's had been. This man was probably a Pharisee, and his legalistic mind was evidently more interested in heaping burdens on people than in seeing them freed by the mercy of Christ.

Christ explicitly pointed out the man's basic problem: religious hypocrisy (Luke 13:15). He had never come to see the weight of guilt he was under. What a call to repentance for this man! Christ was being merciful in confronting him. He could have wiped him off the face of the earth forever for coming against Him, the Lord of glory. We can only hope that this rebuke was blessed to the man's heart. That's what we all need so desperately—for our masks to be taken off and for our sin to be exposed. Only then do we really see ourselves as sinners before God.

Christ also explained how inconsistent this man was. He reminded him that even the Pharisees would make sure their animals were given water on the Sabbath. They would pull one of their sheep out of a pit into which it had fallen on the Sabbath (Matt. 12:11). Thus, says Christ, "ought not this woman, being a daughter of Abraham, whom Satan hath bound, lo, these eighteen years, be loosed from this bond on the sabbath day?" (Luke 13:16). In other words: If the needs of animals are met on the Sabbath, shouldn't the needs of this woman have been met?

Before we condemn this leader of the synagogue, let's examine our hearts. Do we have real love and concern for those carrying impossible burdens? Are we concerned with those in our "synagogues" who are bearing heavy loads? Paul instructs us to bear one another's burdens and so fulfill the law of Christ (Gal. 6:2). This ruler of the synagogue didn't seem to care much for this woman, or he would have rejoiced with her and glorified God with her when he saw her burden lifted.

Thus, this passage illustrates a deep contrast. Christ raises up those who, as this woman, are bowed down in anguish (see Ps. 146:8). On the other hand, those who proudly resist the Lord, as this ruler of the synagogue did, are turned upside down (see Ps. 146:9). It is only when we rest in His mercy that we begin to enjoy a true Sabbath.

Questions

1. Christ seemed intentionally to pick the Sabbath for many of His miracles (e.g., Matt. 12:10; Mark 1:21–28; John 5:9; 9:14). What can we learn from Jesus about how to use the Sabbath?

2. It is not unusual for people to come to a house of worship burdened—perhaps not physically, but emotionally or spiritually. What are some of the burdens that people can carry with them into the house of God?

3. In what way does this woman's physical condition picture the spiritual problem of a fallen sinner? Consult Psalm 38.

4. Compare and contrast the woman and the ruler of the synagogue. Why would it have been so much easier for the ruler to endure the woman's suffering for eighteen years than her healing?

5. Christ implied that this man had more concern for his animals than for this woman. What are some ways you could show concern for burdened people around you more than perhaps your possessions?

20

The Healing of Bartimaeus

Mark 10:46–52

Jesus said unto him, Go thy way: thy faith hath made thee whole.
—MARK 10:52

On His last trip through Jericho, shortly before His crucifixion, Christ had merciful dealings with two very different people: Bartimaeus and Zacchaeus (see Luke 19:1–10). Bartimaeus was a beggar; Zacchaeus was a rich tax collector. All Bartimaeus could do was receive; Zacchaeus did plenty of taking. Bartimaeus met with pity from people; Zacchaeus, disdain. Yet both of these men were objects of Christ's seeking love and mercy who stand as glorious trophies displaying what the powerful grace of Christ can do. They were two of His last converts as He entered Jerusalem to suffer and die.

Let's focus now specifically on the miracle Christ did for the first of these, blind Bartimaeus.

A Blind Beggar

As Jesus went through Jericho on His way to the Passover feast in Jerusalem, He was joined by crowds of people. But Scripture focuses our attention on one man, Bartimaeus.

Mark explains that this name means "son of Timaeus." Timaeus literally means "honorable" or "highly prized," reminiscent of the words of Isaiah 43:4: "Since thou wast precious in my sight, thou hast been honourable, and I have loved thee." When we first meet him, though, Bartimaeus is far from being in an honorable position. Instead, he was a needy man.

- *He needed money.* His stretched-out hand symbolizes this need. He had to beg for the basic necessities of life. In our culture, those who are blind are able to work in various capacities and can live independent or semi-independent lives. But Bartimaeus was forced to beg for his livelihood.

- *He needed help.* Unable to make his way around on his own, Bartimaeus was dependent on those around him. Their kindness to him made it possible for him to move around.

- *He needed sight.* We aren't told how long Bartimaeus had been blind, so we don't know whether he ever knew what it was to see. But he longed for sight. How different his life would be if he could see!

We can imagine what a hardship it would be to be blind. But do we realize that the entire human race has suffered from a different kind of blindness—the lack of spiritual sight? We are blinded because of sin. We used to walk in the light of life in fellowship with our Creator; however, when we fell from Him in disobedience, the light of our understanding was darkened (Eph. 4:18). As a result, by nature we are all spiritually helpless and hopeless. We lack the honor we once had, and, instead, we are pictures of poverty, shame, and disgrace.

By nature, none of us realizes our spiritual blindness— and that is the worst part of our misery. We imagine that we see fine and that our view of reality is accurate. We assume that our eyes aren't bad; we don't realize the spiritual darkness we are under, and therefore no one by nature is begging for spiritual things as Bartimaeus did for his sight. He, at least, knew he was blind! Instead, like the Laodiceans, we live as if we were "rich, and increased with goods, and have need of nothing," not realizing that we are "wretched, and miserable, and poor, and blind, and naked" (Rev. 3:17). The truth is, we are profoundly in need of light, life, and faith. What a blessing that Bartimaeus had been given faith (Luke 18:42)!

A Believing Cry

After He healed Bartimaeus, Jesus would make clear that he had received spiritual sight before he received physical sight. Let's learn some things about the faith of Bartimaeus.

- *Bartimaeus believed that Jesus was the promised Messiah.* This is clear from Luke 18:36–38. At a certain point, a crowd passed by Bartimaeus. Hearing the commotion, he asked what was happening. We don't know what Bartimaeus had heard about Jesus before this point or what he knew from the Old Testament about the coming Messiah. But he knew enough to call Jesus the son of David. This was a way of referring to the Messiah, for the Old Testament prophesied that He would come from the family of David.

- *Bartimaeus was persuaded that Christ could give him the mercy he needed.* The Lord tested Bartimaeus's faith, as He does in the life of all believers. The word used in the original makes clear that because Jesus did not seem to hear him at first, Bartimaeus kept on crying, perhaps for ten or twenty minutes—or even longer. The crowds of people began to rebuke him, "that he should hold his peace" (Luke 18:39). But none of these obstacles could silence Bartimaeus. He continued crying out for mercy. What a lesson for us! There are obstacles in the way to Christ, and we can sometimes become disheartened. Yet, like Jacob at Peniel, we need to keep saying to the Lord: "I will not let thee go, except thou bless me" (Gen. 32:26).

Bartimaeus had learned a few things from begging by the roadside. His ears had to be alert to hear people as they came near. He had learned that he had to stick his hand out there, in people's faces. He must have known, as well, that there was little use in trying to put on a good front. In fact, the more miserable and wretched he looked, the more pity he would receive from passersby. He just had to throw his misery out there, so to speak, without apology and without excuse—as nasty as it was—and wait for someone to have mercy on him. There was nothing to lose, but everything to gain. Let us be encouraged by this to bare our souls to the Lord in all our need and misery!

- *Bartimaeus's faith made the Lord Jesus stand still.*
True faith will always end up at the feet of the
Savior. We don't know when the Holy Spirit
had worked faith in the heart of Bartimaeus, but
clearly the Father had sent the Spirit, and the
Spirit had opened Bartimaeus's closed heart, soft-
ening his will and showing him his need for mercy.
That is clear when we look at John 6:44, where
Jesus tells the complaining Jews that no one can
come to Him unless the Father draws him. And
those who are drawn will come to Him in faith!
And they will reach Him, for He will stand still to
hear and answer them.

A Merciful Savior

These are truly amazing words: "Jesus stood still" (Mark
10:49). The Son of God stood still for a poor, blind beggar!
He didn't stand still to rebuke Bartimaeus. He didn't stand
still to ask that Bartimaeus be gotten out of His way. He
didn't stand still to give Bartimaeus a few coins to make it
through the week. Instead, we read that He "commanded
him to be called." Christ stood still to show mercy. No wonder the people said, "Be of good comfort, rise; he calleth thee"
(Mark 10:49). What a comfort for Bartimaeus—he had been
calling Jesus, but now Jesus was calling him!

Bartimaeus obeyed the Lord's call immediately and
eagerly. We read that he cast away in haste his garment—
something probably long and like a tunic (Mark 10:50).
Anything that would impede our progress in running to
Jesus needs to go.

Christ then asked Bartimaeus what it was that he wanted from Him. How would you answer that question? Many would be content if Christ would give them an easier life, physical health, help with their problems, or more comfortable circumstances. When the Lord brings us to Himself, we can and may ask Him for any and all things in accordance with His will. Bartimaeus vocalized his most pressing need: "Lord, that I might receive my sight" (Mark 10:51). Is spiritual sight your most pressing need?

It was Mercy in the flesh that asked this question and then listened to Bartimaeus's answer. It was Mercy in the flesh that gave him what he asked for and drove away the darkness from his life. It was Mercy that shone like a bright light, kindling inner sight in Bartimaeus's life. How great the mercy of the Son of God!

What do you think Bartimaeus saw first after his healing? I believe that it was not the sun, people, flowers, or trees around him on which he focused his gaze. Wouldn't he wish to see his Great Physician's face first? He looked into the face of the true Son of Honor—Christ Jesus. He looked at the One who not only had made the trees and the flowers but also who was willing to walk the whole way of suffering, beyond Jericho and on to Calvary, to shed His blood for him and for others such as him. Because of Christ's work on the cross, there would be light for those who sit in darkness (Isa. 9:2). Because of Calvary, Psalm 34:5 could be true: "They looked unto him, and were lightened: and their faces were not ashamed."

It is hardly a surprise that Bartimaeus wanted to follow Jesus: "Immediately he received his sight, and followed Jesus in the way" (Mark 10:52). Jesus was the light of the world. Light attracts, and Bartimaeus wanted to walk in the light as He is in the light, for then we have fellowship with Him (1 John 1:7).

We don't know how long Bartimaeus stayed with Jesus. Could it be that he watched the Savior suffering on the cross or was one of those to whom Jesus appeared after His resurrection? We can safely assume that until his dying day he continued as a disciple of Christ, following the Master who had bestowed such mercy upon him.

Questions

1. For further study: you can read about this miracle in Luke 18:35–43 also.

2. What did the prophets predict Messiah would do with the blind (see, e.g., Isa. 42:6–7)? What hope is there in this miracle for those who are spiritually blind today?

3. Bartimaeus faced a number of hindrances. What hindrances do you face in your life that seem to keep you from feeling the nearness of the Lord Jesus?

4. Notice how wide open Christ's question is for Bartimaeus: "What wilt thou that I shall do unto thee?" (Luke 18:51). What does this say about Christ's heart today? What sorts of things may we ask from Him?

5. Why do you think Jesus told Bartimaeus that his faith had saved him (Luke 18:42)? How might that be useful to Bartimaeus later on as well as to us today?

6. Compare Luke 18:43 with John 10:4. Can we have spiritual light and not follow the Lord Jesus? If you are following Him, put into your own words what it means to follow Him today.

21

The Withered Fig Tree

Mark 11:11–26

> *Peter... saith unto him, Master, behold, the fig tree which*
> *thou cursedst is withered away. And Jesus answering saith*
> *unto them, Have faith in God.*
> —MARK 11:21–22

Mark 11 records events that took place during the last week
of Christ's ministry on earth—a week filled with both ten-
sion and expectation. At one point, Christ overlooked the
city of Jerusalem and wept (Luke 19:41–42). At another, He
was overthrowing the tables of the moneychangers (Mark
11:15–17). In these final days of His ministry, Christ con-
ducted Himself as if He were walking on the edge of the
fierce judgment that He would endure. All He said and did
pertained to this truth either as a message of weal or woe.
Some scenes are exuberant; others, solemn.

One such solemn scene is Christ's miracle of the withered fig tree. We should note that although Christ's power
was usually revealed in miracles of *mercy*, this was a miracle
of *judgment*. While Christ had often restored the withered
bodies of disabled people (Matt. 12:13; John 5:8; Acts 3:7),
in Mark 11 He withered a fruitless tree. We considered

Christ's only other miracle with an element of judgment in chapter 9—when a legion of demons was cast into a herd of swine that then plunged themselves into the lake (Mark 5:13). Even in that miracle, however, the main purpose was the healing of the demon-possessed man. So this certainly is a unique miracle with a unique message.

Understanding the Miracle

We can surmise from a number of passages that Christ was lodging at this time in Bethany, which was located on the Mount of Olives, just a short walking distance from the city of Jerusalem (Mark 11:1, 11). This miracle most likely took place on the Monday before what we know today as Good Friday. The day before, Christ had entered the city, welcomed by the Hosanna cries of the children (Mark 11:1–10). When He arrived at the temple, He "looked round about upon all things" (Mark 11:11). This quiet, solemn inspection of the temple by the Son of God must have been impressive to those who observed it.

Early the next morning, the Savior walked toward Jerusalem. He was hungry (Mark 11:12). We don't know if he had been fasting or had missed a morning meal, but along the road were many fig trees. In fact, Bethphage (referred to in Mark 11:1), a neighboring village to Bethany, means "the house of figs." If the figs were ripe, people passing by along the road would often help themselves to them.

There were basically three times a year when ripe figs could be found on trees—June, August, and December. It was now only March or early April; Mark says "the time of figs was not yet" (11:13). But even this early in the year a small fruit could be found on the fig tree before the leaves came out. This small fruit was knob-like and starchy tasting. Solomon is probably referring to this fruit in Song of Solomon 2:13, in his description of early spring: "The fig tree putteth forth her green figs." Ancient literature tells us that peasants might eat this fruit when they were hungry; otherwise, it would fall off later, when the real fruit would begin to form.

As the Savior approached, He saw a fig tree with leaves on it. He came up to it "if haply he might find" some fruit on it, but He found "nothing but leaves" (Mark 11:13). Thereupon He pronounced the following curse: "No man eat fruit of thee hereafter for ever" (Mark 11:14). The Lord Jesus' words produced a dramatic result. Matthew 21:19 tells us, "Presently the fig tree withered away." Mark tells us what Jesus and His disciples saw as they came past the place the next day: "the fig tree dried up from the roots" (11:20).

Was Christ acting harshly when He cursed this tree, as some commentators suggest? Was this an unwarranted act of frustration on His part? Let's remember first that Jesus Christ is the Creator of everything, including all the trees of the field. They are His to do with as He pleases. God gave Adam dominion over the fish, the birds, and the trees of the field (Gen. 1:28). Shouldn't Christ as the second Adam be able to exercise that dominion? Also, let us not forget that this Lord Jesus was perfectly sinless. Hebrews 7:26 describes Him as "holy, harmless, undefiled." His speech was always sinless: "Neither was guile found in his mouth" (1 Peter 2:22). Surely, especially as the time came near for Him to bear the curse of God's wrath against sin, His actions and words were neither arbitrary nor insignificant.

The Lord's Searching Gaze

This miracle of Christ has a profoundly spiritual meaning. The Old Testament often compares people to trees, as in Psalm 1:3, for example. More specifically, Israel, or the church of the Old Testament, is compared frequently to a fig tree (e.g., Hos. 9:10). This means that the Lord expects us to produce fruit, and, as Lord, He is entitled to the fruit of what He has planted. In fact, in Micah 7 the Lord pictures Himself as one who desires to eat the fruit produced by His people, but "there is no cluster to eat: my soul desired the firstripe fruit" (v. 1). Christ Himself points to this same principle in the parable of the fig tree (Luke 13:6–9).

The text implies that there were many fruitless and leafless trees along the road that day, but Christ did not curse any of them. So the problem with this particular tree was not its fruitlessness, but rather that it seemed to pretend to have fruit, whereas the others did not. In other words, this must have been a beautiful tree whose boughs gave an impression of fruitfulness.

The Bible teaches that "man looketh on the outward appearance, but the LORD looketh on the heart" (1 Sam. 16:7). Just as the Lord Jesus examined this tree from top to bottom and looked under its leaves to see if there was any fruit, so He examines the hearts and lives of men. Jeremiah 17:10 tells us: "I the LORD search the heart, I try the reins." Sadly, He often sees only leaves and no fruit.

For what fruit is the Lord looking? The Bible clearly teaches us which sacrifices God accepts: poor and contrite hearts that tremble at the word; repentance toward God and faith in the Lord Jesus Christ; love for Christ; love for souls;

hatred of sin; contentment in God and the lot He gives us in life; longing for Him and His righteousness; liberality to the poor; resting in Christ and His finished work; renouncing the hidden things of dishonesty (Ps. 51:17). Christ is looking for the fruit of the Spirit, which "is love, joy, peace, longsuffering, gentleness, goodness, faith, meekness, temperance" (Gal. 5:22–23).

We should remember that Christ had just been in the temple. The next day, He would go there again and would find a parallel to this fig tree in a remarkable way. It was a stunning and impressive temple, with magnificently dressed priests, imposing Pharisees, and rich people giving gifts in showy ways—but all these things were just beautiful leaves without real fruit.

The Lord's Withering Words

Focus for a moment on the cutting words the Savior speaks to this tree: "No man eat fruit of thee hereafter for ever" (Mark 11:14). None of us could accomplish anything by speaking to a tree, but Christ's word can both give life and take it away. The effect of His withering words fulfilled Ezekiel 17:24: "All the trees of the field shall know that I the LORD have brought down the high tree, have exalted the low tree, *have dried up the green tree*, and have made the dry tree to flourish: I the LORD have spoken and·have done it" (emphasis added).

What are we to learn from this withering fig tree? One lesson for us is that coming to Christ is difficult, especially for religious people. We love our beautiful fig leaves too much. Like Adam and Eve, we use our fig leaves to cover up our shame and sin. God needs to expose our sin and show that all our excuses and efforts to cover it up are vain. One of the main purposes of preaching is to uncover the false show of religion in our lives. This is the Holy Spirit's work through the word still today: "And when he is come, he will reprove the world of sin, and of righteousness, and of judgment" (John 16:8).

This is exactly what happened with Saul of Tarsus. If anyone had a beautifully leafy fig tree of a life, it was Saul. Yet with Christ's utterance of one word from heaven, Saul's religion withered before him (Acts 9:3–6) until nothing was left, and he appeared as he truly was. Paul expressed it like this: "I died" (Rom. 7:9). He died to his self-righteous religion in order to be made alive in Christ to bear true fruit. Then, and only then, would he bear real fruit.

If the Lord does not show us our fruitlessness in the day of grace, He will do it in the day of judgment. Then before angels and devils and the whole world, He will show how we should have produced fruit to His glory and honor, but we didn't. Then the sentence of His judgment will come down on countless people who trusted that all was well. With the word of His mouth, He will send them away.

The Lord's Unmatched Beauty

It would be helpful to take a moment to compare this fruitless fig tree with what the Bible describes as a truly fruitful tree. Actually, the Lord Jesus Himself is the best picture. A few days later, He would compare Himself to a "green" or living tree and Jerusalem to a "dry" or lifeless tree (Luke 23:31).

Indeed, has anyone ever seen a more beautiful and fruitful tree than He? Heaven's verdict of Him was "this is my beloved Son, in whom I am well pleased" (Matt. 17:5). Never was there such matchless beauty! But despite His being a glorious Tree, heaven would pronounce a curse on Him just three days after these events. He would be "made a curse" (Gal. 3:13) and enter an infinitely greater judgment than this tree. The tree lost only the plant life it had, but nothing more. By His death on the cross, Christ endured eternal death for each one of His people.

But three days later, in the garden of Joseph of Arimathaea, this tree appeared with "the power of an endless life" (Heb. 7:16). He is all the more radiant and beautiful now. He lives forevermore—and because He lives, His people can live also (John 14:19). That's the gospel of free grace. In the gospel, He calls both unrighteous and self-righteous sinners to Himself.

By nature, you and I are like this fruitless fig tree. We must not be satisfied with having leaves without any real fruit. Let us seek the Lord Jesus Christ. In and through Him alone we can bear fruit pleasing to God: "From me is thy fruit found" (Hos. 14:8). This Savior yields His fruit continually, without fail, and to the satisfaction of every hungry sinner (Rev. 22:2). Under every leaf of this tree is abundant fruit for even the most wretched and needy sinner: "He that cometh to me shall never hunger" (John 6:35).

Not only does He supply the *greatest* benefits, He can save *to the uttermost*, "seeing he ever liveth" (Heb. 7:25). The same Christ who said "die" to the fig tree can also say "live." How important it is for believers to cling to this Christ! We don't find the life of our own hand (see Isa. 57:10). Instead, the Lord Jesus says, "He that abideth in me, and I in him, the same bringeth forth much fruit" (John 15:5).

Questions

1. For further study: you can read about this miracle in Mark 11:11–26 also.

2. Why is a "fig leaf" religion so powerful and prevalent? What are some of the ways we can cover ourselves up with a good-looking veneer?

3. What would you say to someone who says that the church is full of hypocrites?

4. What fruits are we supposed to bear? Would you agree that it is easier to see fruit in others than in yourself? Why or why not?

5. Why does Christ point Peter to the need for faith in God (Mark 11:22)? What does faith have to do with what Christ has been speaking of? You may want to consult with a good commentary (such as those by John Calvin, Matthew Henry, Matthew Poole, or J. C. Ryle) on this.

6. How do we find the opposite of hypocrisy in Christ? Why is He so necessary if we wish to be finished with a veneer religion? If you are in these circumstances, are you prepared for what He might do in your life? If you can, write about what God did to unmask hypocrisy in your life.

22

The Healing of Malchus's Ear

Luke 22:39–53

And one of them smote the servant of the high priest, and cut off his right ear. And Jesus answered and said, Suffer ye thus far. And he touched his ear, and healed him.
—LUKE 22:50–51

Healing Malchus's ear is the last miracle Christ performed during His earthly ministry before His death. Perhaps at first glance the healing of an ear doesn't seem to be a magnificent final miracle. Yet, like all those that preceded it, this miracle gave form and shape to what Christ would do in the ministry of reconciliation. It was also a great bridge to what Christ would do in His state of exaltation following His death and resurrection.

A Sword-Wielding Disciple

Christ had come to the garden of Gethsemane to pray. Receiving no help in prayer from His disciples, the Savior accepted the cup of His Father and prepared to meet the power of darkness.

Led by Judas and armed with swords, clubs, and torches, a band of about two hundred soldiers and temple guards arrived in Gethsemane. Christ revealed His royal dignity to them as the Son of God, forcing the soldiers backward to the ground (John 18:4–7). Nevertheless, He then allowed these soldiers to bind His hands—hands that had healed the sick, blessed children, and done so many other miracles (John 18:8–12). But before being bound, Jesus would do one last act of healing with those blessed hands on an enemy who had come to seize Him.

In the darkness, the blade of a sword suddenly swung through the air. Had some soldier from the temple guard gone on attack? No, one of the Lord's disciples reached for his sword and pulled it out of its sheath. He lunged toward the group and aimed for the head of one of the soldiers. Perhaps in the dim light the victim saw the shining blade coming his way and, throwing his weight to one side, managed to avoid having his head cut off. Instead, the sword took off the victim's ear. John tells us that the victim's name was Malchus and that he was a servant of the high priest, Caiaphas.

Imagine Malchus reaching for the right side of his head to find his ear gone and his head bleeding profusely. John says that the perpetrator of this crime was Simon Peter, known for his impetuous words and actions. What did this sword-wielding disciple's action accomplish? Was he helping his Lord here? No, Peter had done damage to both Malchus and to his Lord. Christ had just said in Peter's hearing: "Let these go their way" (John 18:8). Peter should have taken this as a cue that what was going to happen would not involve him, but instead of getting *out* of the way, he got *in* the way. His sword dripping with blood, he was more ready for Armageddon than for the Passion.

We often respond like Peter did when we see more of the enemy around us than we do the guilt within us. We are so easily persuaded to see Christianity as a cause in which we must fight. We see the many enemies who threaten us; we become very anxious and perhaps even angry when we see the cause of evil advancing. But we should remember that Christianity is not, in sum and substance, a cause to be fought outside of us as much as it is a work of grace within us. That grace causes us to rest in the finished work of Christ. If we had to add one sword stroke to the cause of our salvation, we would be lost forever.

No wonder, then, that the Lord admonished Peter: "Put up thy sword into the sheath" (John 18:11). Scripture elsewhere teaches the lesson as follows: "Be not overcome of evil, but overcome evil with good" (Rom. 12:21). This is not the time for fighting. "The weapons of our warfare are not carnal, but mighty through God" (2 Cor. 10:4). More importantly, you can't share the work with the Mediator.

Has the Lord shown you that you are too quick to wield a sword—not necessarily a physical sword, but the "sword" of your tongue, look, temper, and impetuous actions that get in the Lord's way? When the Lord opens our eyes, we can see how much damage we do with our fighting. Even in the church and spiritual communities there is much sword swinging from which we must repent and turn.

Peter would have no one to blame but himself if his discipleship and ministry had ended right at this point. What a mercy it didn't! This was owing to Christ as the merciful High Priest.

A Merciful High Priest

Among the gospel authors, it was the physician Luke who described this miracle of the heavenly Physician. We read in Luke 22:51, "He touched his ear, and healed him." That must have meant that Christ bent down and picked up the ear and put it right back where it had been. His touch tenderly yet powerfully restored the tissues, muscles, and nerves, bringing healing to Malchus.

We see Christ as the merciful High Priest in two ways. He was a *High Priest toward Peter*. Peter couldn't be left to himself for one moment. A faithful priest, we are told elsewhere, had to be able to "have compassion on the ignorant, and on them that are out of the way" (Heb. 5:2). And that is exactly how Christ intervened with His erring disciple. He would undo what Peter had done. The messianic Psalm 69 sheds light on what Christ was doing here: "Then I restored that which I took not away" (v. 4). Peter had cut off Malchus's ear, but Christ restored it. This pictures what Christ's work on the cross would be like. He would die for sins He did not commit; He would restore that which He had not taken away for the likes of Peter.

At the same time, He was a merciful *High Priest toward Malchus*. Malchus was the servant of Caiaphas, the earthly high priest descending from the line of Aaron. We know Caiaphas's track record, and from it we can deduce what a sad life Malchus must have lived in the shadow of this corrupt and vain high priest. But now a perfect high priest, Jesus, a priest after the order of Melchisedec whose blood was about to be shed as a suffering substitute, would bind up his wound. Christ did not think an ear too small a thing through which to make a final display of His miraculous power during His earthly ministry. Before having His high priestly hands bound and going to the cross, He was using them to show kindness to an enemy. What a merciful High Priest!

A Healed Ear

We don't know whether Malchus ever came to believe in and live for this merciful High Priest, Jesus Christ. Because he is explicitly mentioned in John, a book written some fifty years after the events it records, some commentators surmise that his name may have lived on in the Christian community as someone who had come into the Lord's service. Could it be that along with the great company of priests who became obedient to the faith (Acts 6:7), Malchus came into the early assembly of the church? We won't know for sure until eternity.

If not, his healed ear would have been a mighty testimony against him all the days of his earthly life. The Lord had done a wonder on him, but where had that brought him? How many wonders has the Lord done in our lives, including in our physical bodies? These are strong calls to us to abandon a formal religion like the kind Caiaphas represented.

Meanwhile, the healed ear of Malchus was a testimony to Peter of Christ's healing power through His dying and rising. We know that he learned the lesson, for he wrote later,

> For this is thankworthy, if a man for conscience toward God endure grief, suffering wrongfully. For what glory is it, if, when ye be buffeted for your faults, ye shall take it patiently? but if, when ye do well, and suffer for it, ye take it patiently, this is

acceptable with God. For even hereunto were ye called: because Christ also suffered for us, leaving us an example, that ye should follow his steps.... When he suffered, he threatened not; but committed himself to him that judgeth righteously: who his own self bare our sins in his own body on the tree, that we, being dead to sins, should live unto righteousness: by whose stripes ye were healed. (1 Peter 2:19–24)

Peter went on to preach of Jesus Christ as the spiritual healer and restorer. On the day of Pentecost, he showed that the sword of the kingdom is a *spiritual* sword. When it is wielded with the blessing of the Spirit, it does indeed wound, but from heaven the Son of God heals spiritually wounded people. What a blessing that Peter could continue as a servant of the real High Priest, Jesus, proclaiming His love and mercy to those enslaved to sin and formal religion.

Questions

1. For further study: you can read about this miracle in John 18:1–11 also.

2. According to Luke 22:49, the disciples asked the Lord whether they should attack with the sword. Peter didn't seem to wait for an answer (v. 50). What lesson can we learn from this about waiting on the Lord and not deciding ourselves what the Lord wants us to do?

3. Earlier, in the garden of Gethsemane, Peter had failed to watch and pray as Christ had told him to. Now he did what he shouldn't have done. How does Peter represent believers who, though well-intentioned, are still often so thoughtless? Compare also what he said in Luke 22:33 and 60.

4. Why does the heart of a disciple still often continue to have such difficulty with the way of suffering—both Christ's suffering and his own? What did Peter learn according to 1 Peter 2:19–24?

5. Malchus served the high priest Caiaphas. Peter was the servant of Christ, the true High Priest. Compare and contrast these lines of service.

6. Spiritually speaking, Christ wounds our hearts by the law and then heals them in the gospel. How did He do this in the life of Peter (think of his denial and restoration) and Paul (think of his conversion)?

23

The Resurrection

Matthew 28:1–10

The angel answered…, Fear not ye: for I know that ye seek Jesus, which was crucified. He is not here: for he is risen, as he said. Come, see the place where the Lord lay.
—MATTHEW 28:5–6

We have looked at a number of the miracles that Christ performed during His earthly ministry. But His miracles were not limited to His time on earth. After His ascension, He performed miracles from heaven through His apostles. For example, the lame man at the gate Beautiful was healed by the power of Christ's name (Acts 3:16). And through power given to them by Christ, Peter raised Dorcas from the dead (Acts 9:40), and Paul later raised Eutychus from the dead (Acts 20:10–11).

Christ's coming to this world and leaving it also involved miracles. The incarnation of Christ through the virgin birth was a great miracle (Matt. 1:23; John 1:14). The ascension into heaven could also be classified as a miracle, as Christ was bodily received into heaven (Acts 1:9–10).

As we conclude this look at the miracles, however, I want to focus our attention on a pivotal miracle that, we could

say, undergirds all the miracles we have looked at so far—
the miracle of Christ's resurrection from the dead. As Paul
said, without Christ's resurrection from the dead, we would
be "of all men most miserable" (1 Cor. 15:19). We can all
understand that if Christ had been only a miracle worker,
and nothing more, the gospel would be a pitiful thing. He
did not come only to alleviate suffering and pain for a while.
He came with a much greater mission—to save His people
from their sin, misery, and death by dying on the cross and
rising again. So as glorious as Christ's miracles during His
ministry were, none of them comes close to the miracle on
which the church stands and to which it owes its existence.
Without the resurrection, nothing else would make sense.
And so Christ's miraculous works could be said to both *flow
from* Christ's resurrection and *point to* it.

The Place of This Miracle

We cannot properly appreciate the miracle of the resurrection unless we understand the significance of its setting. The
previous miracles we looked at were performed in places such
as synagogues, in houses, on the sea, in crowds, on the grassy
landscape—all common, everyday backdrops for ordinary
life. No miracles had occurred *in the grave*—a place that
could be considered the home of death. The raising of the
young man of Nain took place as he was being carried *to* his
grave (Luke 7:14). Another miracle (one in the gospel of John
that we haven't looked at in this book) took place as Lazarus
was called *out* of his grave (11:43–44). Even then, however,
Christ, the Resurrection and the Life, stood *outside* Lazarus's grave and called him *from* it. The miracle of Christ's

resurrection, however, took place *inside* a sealed sepulcher that had a stone in front of it. This is an amazing fact. Graves are monuments to the power of death. Apart from the truth of redeeming grace, every gravestone could be seen as a victory marker for death because of sin.

If Christ had not risen from the dead, the tomb in Joseph of Arimathaea's garden would represent greater misery than all other tombs combined. For not just death would have triumphed there—Christ's tomb would also represent the devil's triumph and the death of all hope. Remember how hopeless the travelers on the road to Emmaus felt after Christ's crucifixion? They were so disappointed by His death, for they "trusted that it had been he which should have redeemed Israel" (Luke 24:21). That same hopelessness would be ours if it were not for the resurrection of the crucified Lord. For then there would be no hope of salvation!

With the exception of His cursing of the fig tree, every one of Christ's miracles reversed, or turned back, some aspect of the curse that has come into the world because of sin. Whether it delivered from leprosy, blindness, hunger, storms, injury, or death, each of Christ's miracles brought restoration and blessing to a situation of need, and profound happiness in exchange for sorrow. Think of Jairus's family after his daughter had been raised, or of the widow of Nain after her son had been brought back to life, or of Mary and Martha after Lazarus had been given back to them. What incredible joy these people must have felt! What a transformation because of what Christ was able to do!

But after His crucifixion, Christ's body was laid in the tomb. All seemed lost! No wonder the disciples and the women were pictures of despondency on the eve of the resurrection. And yet the Son of God had not surrendered any of His offices, though His body lay lifeless in the tomb.[10] The miracle-working Christ would rise again through a miracle greater than any they had seen.

The Agent of the Resurrection

There were no human witnesses at the actual moment of the resurrection, although more than five hundred people saw the Lord after He had arisen (1 Cor. 15:6). Who, then, raised Jesus from the dead? We can be sure that it was not the angels who raised Him. They rolled away the stone in order that the women and disciples could look inside the empty tomb, but they did not roll away the stone to let Christ *out* of the tomb. That was something the angels would have been incapable of.

Scripture makes abundantly clear that it was the triune God who effected the resurrection. First, the Father raised Jesus from the dead (Acts 2:24; 3:15; 10:40; Eph. 1:20). In doing so the Father showed that He accepted His Son's work and person. Romans 6:4 puts it beautifully: "Christ was raised up from the dead by the glory of the Father." What a splendid truth that is! We think of Abraham, the Old Testament patriarch, who, figuratively speaking, received his beloved son Isaac back from the dead (Heb. 11:19). Abraham hadn't raised Isaac from the dead, though—he could only *receive* him back. But God the Father did *raise* the body of His Son in our human nature.

The Holy Spirit was also involved in the resurrection. Paul says that Christ was raised by the power of the Spirit (Rom.

8:11; 1 Peter 3:18). In like manner, God's church is brought from death to life by the power of the Spirit (Rom. 8:11).

But it was not only the Father and the Spirit who were active in raising Christ from the dead. The New Testament makes clear that Christ was active, not passive, in His own resurrection. *He* arose! Death could not hold Him captive! He broke its bonds and lives with the power of an endless life. He told His disciples in advance that He would arise (e.g., Matt. 16:21). He told them afterward that He had to arise (e.g., Luke 24:46). Paul tells us that "he rose again the third day" (1 Cor. 15:4).

Notice that Christ spoke of His resurrection as the *taking* of His life again in John 10:17–18: "Therefore doth my Father love me, because I lay down my life, that I might take it again. No man taketh it from me, but I lay it down of myself. I have power to lay it down, and I have power to take it again. This commandment have I received of my Father." Just as life was not taken *from* Christ without His ready and willing consent, so too life was not given *to* Him again without His consent and activity.

One of the reasons that Christ died was to rise again. That is what He means when He says, "Therefore doth my Father love me, because I lay down my life, *that* I might take it again" (John 10:17, emphasis added). He was willing—even eager—to die in order that He might rise again and be the victor over death.

Clearly, then, Christ appears more glorious in the miracle of His resurrection than in any other miracle. He laid down His life in order that He might take it again as a public person, as the second Adam, as the Head of His church. What

delight it gave Him to do that for His Father's glory. As He
performed other miracles, He turned back devils, disease, and
death, acting on these forces as they were *around* Him. But in
the miracle of His resurrection, He Himself entered *into* the
domain of death and plundered it. In His death and resurrection, He secured the proper foundation for the redemptive
message of which His other miracles had testified.

The Fruit of the Resurrection

The miracle of the resurrection brings many blessings to
Christ's church and people. It is incredibly hope giving, purpose giving, and prospect giving. It gives the church a gospel
to preach. It gives His people a living Lord in heaven and a
Holy Spirit present in them to apply the resurrection's benefits to them. What comfort the resurrection gives when we
face death! Lord's Day 17 of the Heidelberg Catechism summarizes the benefits of Christ's resurrection this way:

> *Q. What doth the resurrection of Christ profit us?*
>
> A. First, by His resurrection He has overcome death,
> that He might make us partakers of that righteous-
> ness which He had purchased for us by His death;
> secondly, we are also by His power raised up to a new
> life; and lastly, the resurrection of Christ is a sure
> pledge of our blessed resurrection.

Let's consider this beautiful answer in more detail.

The first major benefit, then, is that by His resurrection,
Christ has purchased a righteousness that can stand before the
tribunal of God. By a life of obedience as a public person, as
a representative of His people, He obtained a righteousness,

which we call His active obedience. By His suffering and death on the cross, He took the curse of sin, paid the price for sin, and satisfied the justice of God that had been provoked by sinners. In the resurrection, He shows all of this as righteousness that God approves of that can be credited to sinners. He not only obtained that righteousness, but, by His resurrection, He now has a life whereby He can apply that righteousness through His Holy Spirit (Rom. 4:25).

Second, by His resurrection Christ raises dead sinners to newness of life. Because of our sin we are not only *guilty* before God; we are also *dead* in sins and trespasses. We need to be made alive again by the power of Christ through the Holy Spirit. We need new life in our members by the Holy Spirit. We need Christ to raise us to newness of life every day. Because of His resurrection, He can do this. Because He lives, His people can live also.

Finally, by His resurrection, Christ has gone through death for His people. Death was not able to hold Him—nor will it be able to hold them. It can act only as a passageway into life eternal. Because He rose from the grave on the first day of the week, He has obtained the right to open all the graves on the final day of human history and take all His people to Himself into everlasting life.

In conclusion, I ask you this: Have you experienced the power of this greatest of all miracles in your life? If not, it is time to seek the Lord and repent of your sin. Do not rest till you know the miracle of life from the dead yourself, from the crucified and risen Redeemer. If you have experienced this, the Lord Jesus Christ, the risen One, will be supremely precious to you. You will still experience a struggle with indwelling sin, the body of this death. The devil will continue to assail you, as he does all the children of God. But Satan will never be able to undo the miracle that has been worked in you—the good work that God has begun. Nor can he take the great Miracle Worker off the throne of the universe, for Christ says: "All power is given unto me in heaven and in earth" (Matt. 28:18). The church can answer back to its Lord: "Blessing, and honour, and glory, and power, be unto him that sitteth upon the throne, and unto the Lamb for ever and ever" (Rev. 5:13).

Questions

1. If Christ had simply worked a few miracles, as Elijah and Elisha did, but had not died and risen again, how would things have looked? How should the fact that He died and rose again raise the significance of the resurrection of Christ in our esteem?

2. Why do you think the women were drawn to the grave if they thought Christ was gone forever?

3. What difference does it make that Christ Himself acted in the resurrection?

4. How is life different because of the resurrection?

5. Could justification, sanctification, or glorification be what they are without the resurrection? Trace how the resurrection undergirds these doctrines.

6. How is faith in miracles different from faith in the One who works miracles?

Notes

1. I am planning to write a separate study on the gospel of John, Lord willing.

2. John Calvin, *Commentaries on the Harmony of the Gospels*, trans. William Pringle (Edinburgh: Calvin Translation Society, 1845), 1:242 (Luke 5:8).

3. Charles Haddon Spurgeon, "Carried by Four," in *The Metropolitan Tabernacle Pulpit: Sermons, Parts 189–200* (London: Passmore & Alabaster, 1872), 163, Google e-book.

4. John Newton, "Come, My Soul, Thy Suit Prepare," stanza 2.

5. Edward Hopper, "Jesus, Savior, Pilot Me," stanza 1.

6. Martin Luther, "A Mighty Fortress Is Our God," stanza 3.

7. William Cowper, "God Moves in a Mysterious Way," stanza 3.

8. John Cumming, *Lectures on Our Lord's Miracles* (Philadelphia: Lindsay and Blakiston, 1854), 253.

9. As quoted in Eustace R. Conder, *A Commentary on St. Matthew's Gospel* (London: Paternoster, 1866), 267.

10. John Murray says it well: "We must not then regard the Messianic office or functions as suspended during the period of death and burial. Though dead, he was still the God-man Messiah, and it was in the exercise of such an office that he broke the bands of death and took his life again." "Who Raised Up Jesus?," in *Collected Writings of John Murray* (Edinburgh: Banner of Truth, 1982), 4:89–90.